Lang Fafa Dampha

**West African Nationalism
and Reconstruction**

1

By the same author

i. *Afrique subsaharienne : mémoire, histoire et réparation.* L'Harmattan June 2013.

ii. Reconstruction for Slavery and Colonialism: The Teachings of Durban, Amazon (Createspace), March 2015.

iii. Alien Attitude (novel), CreateSpace, June, 2015.

iv. African Migrants (novel), CreateSpace, August, 2015.

v. Sub-Saharan Africa and the Bretton Woods Institutions, CreateSpace, August, 2015

vi. The United Nations Organisation and African Reconstruction, CreateSpace, August, 2015

In the memory of my late beloved mother-in-law, Aji Ramu Bah, who prematurely passed away on 8 May 2012 just at the age of 58. May the Lord bless your soul.

If we are to remain free, if we are to enjoy the full benefits of Africa's rich resources, we must unite to plan for our total defence and the full exploitation of our material and human means in the full interest of all our people... 'to go it alone' will limit our horizons, curtail our expectations and threaten our liberty.

Osagyefo Dr. Kwame Nkrumah, (Africa Must Unite).

Table of Contents

Introduction

Sub-Saharan Africa suffered centuries of Trans-Saharan and Trans-Atlantic slave trading, followed by about 60 years of European colonisation. A people reduced to slavery, Colonialism and apartheid is a people deprived of their natural unassailable rights. The history of the relationship between Sub-Saharan Africa and the West has shown that its pre-colonial structures were practically dismantled by the institutions of slavery, Colonialism and apartheid. Consequently the African people were deprived of their liberty and sovereignty, because their socio-cultural systems, which had been functioning normally, experienced fundamental transformations. A people's power is determined by the nature and performance of its socio-economic structures and particularly the freedom to decide and manage their own affairs. Slavery and Colonialism made Sub-Saharan Africans lose their power, because they were forced to give way to foreigners, especially the West, the direct properties of their institutions.

The State as a political entity centrally belongs, from a nationalistic outlook, to one large socio-cultural group with the responsibility of preserving its administration and promulgating its traditional norms and values. No society therefore can infinitely bear the direct control of its institutions and its affairs by foreign forces. If it notices the presence of foreign groups trying to dismantle or transform its structures, there are indubitably emerging reactions. The Hottentots and the Bushmen in South Africa strongly resisted European invaders, even if they were in the end overcome. In North America, the thirteen colonies successfully fought against British Imperialism and declared their independence during the American War of Independence.[1] After the settlement of European colonisers and the institution of apartheid in South Africa, Steve Biko, Oliver Tambo, Nelson Mandela and many others continued fighting against the regime until the 1990s when democracy was installed. General Charles de Gaulle in France, aided by some countries, manifestly successfully resisted German occupation in spite of the collaboration of the Vichy government and some of the population with the enemy.

[1] The American War of Independence, the American Revolutionary War (1775–1783), or simply the Revolutionary War in America, began as a war between Great Britain and the thirteen colonies in North America.

With the same fortitude, some leaders in Africa strongly resisted European invasion. The Assante besieged the English in Kumasi, the capital they had occupied, for four months. The great warrior king and founder of the Mandinka (Wassoulou) Empire (1852 - 1882), Almamy Samori Touré waged an eight-year war against the French invaders, manifesting extraordinary tenacity and great military skill. The Baules of Ivory Coast resisted French invasion until 1911; the Igbos of Nigeria were only defeated in 1919; and the Jolas of Senegambia only in the 1920s. In Angola, Chief Ovambo of the Mandumes assembled an army of forty thousand soldiers to resist the Portuguese. German invaders horribly repressed resistance, destroying more than three-quarters of the Herero people and half of the Naja people in German East Africa (Tanganyika) and South-West Africa(Namibia), between 1904 and 1908 (Meredith 3). Even after the coercive institution of the colonial regime in Africa, nationalists with clear vision, and conscious of the objectives of Colonialism, continued to fight against "Western encroachment" especially ideologically. Notwithstanding the fact that, in a military context, Colonialism undermined the existing powers in Africa, resistance continued. During colonisation, Africans were thus conscious of their state as prisoners in their own land, right from the beginning of the colonial invasion, although this awareness was consolidated gradually thanks to the efforts of a group of leaders produced by the colonial system itself.

Every society combating foreign domination thence aspires to liberty and sovereignty in order to effectively govern and control its own affairs. However for this liberty and independence to be meaningful, they have to be linked with sustainable socio-economic progress and prosperity in the society in question. It is against this background that Nationalism and reconstruction[2] in West Africa is studied in this work. Kwame Nkrumah's vision of a liberated Africa was not limited to the expulsion of Colonialism. It incorporated the notion of continental unity that, according to him, was the only way to peace, prosperity and sustainable socio-economic development, and to protect Africans from more potential foreign domination. At this juncture Colonialism was not the only target of Nationalism and

---

[2] In this work, reconstruction carries a broad view referring to the notion of sustainable recovery and development in an African context encompassing all aspects of the society. Its main usage makes reference to the repair of African institutions and systems, but by the efforts of Africans themselves.

reconstruction in Africa, but Imperialism in its larger context which in all circumstances emerges from the sphere of either direct or indirect foreign domination.

We have therefore studied the functioning of the Organisation of African Unity (OAU), as well as its projects at the end of Colonialism, to situate the passage of ideas and the politics of liberation and reconstruction. We have also examined and recalled the errors made by the OAU, to serve as possible lessons for the new African Union (AU). This study has also looked at the two main vehicles of West African Nationalism: Pan-Africanism and Negritude, pioneered by Kwame Nkrumah of Ghana and Léopold Sédar Senghor of Senegal respectively[3], to determine their roles in African reconstruction.

A study of Nationalism in post-colonial Africa would not be complete without considering the aspects of culture and the economy. Yet African Nationalism had been accused of focusing exclusively on the struggle for political independence to the detriment of the economy and especially culture. However the initiative of president Alpha Oumar Konaré of Mali,[4] to establish the Mission for the African Academy of Languages (MACALAN), that was subsequently transformed into the African Academy of Languages (ACALAN) by the Khartoum Decision[5] of 2006, as a supplementary instrument of reconstruction, as well as the institution of the various Regional Economic Communities on the African continent, were attempts to remedy these shortcomings. This work has hence, as well, looked into the cultural and economic aspects of African Nationalism

---

[3]There were many prominent actors of post-colonial Nationalism in West Africa such as Namdi Azikiwe of Nigeria, Sékou Touré of Guinea (Conakry), Houphouët-Boigny of Ivory Coast, Modibo Keita of Mali etc. The nationalistic stance of all these protagonists is affiliated to either Pan-Africanism or Négritude; for this simple reason we have confined ourselves to studying Senghorian Negritude and the Pan-Africanism of Nkrumah.

[4]President Alpha Oumar Konaré was subsequently elected Chairperson of the African Union Commission for the period 2003 and 2008.

[5]The Khartoum Decision was made in 2006, at the summit of the Heads of State and Government of the Member States of the African Union in Khartoum, in which the leaders decided to link culture and education. The Statutes of the African Academy of Languages were also adopted during this summit.

particularly reflecting on the roles played by African languages, and the socio-economic activities of the Economic Community of West African States (ECOWAS), to appraise the effect of the African Renaissance as a tool for effective reconstruction. The importance of the role of culture, especially languages in African reconstruction, has subsequently led us to explore the twin post-colonial associations, namely the Commonwealth of Nations and the *Organisation International de la Francophonie*, and their effect on African culture and especially the development of African languages, as well as on socio-economic development in Africa in general. The activities of these institutions are measured in nationalistic and scientific perspectives, by linking them to the global context of reconstruction in Africa which is the primary function and objective of the African Union.

This work is oriented towards West Africa, particularly English West Africa. However, intermittent references have been made to the whole of Africa, because the nature of African history in this era of post-Colonialism is that specific regions, notably Sub-Saharan Africa, could hardly be effectively studied without considering the whole of the continent.

Chapter one

The concepts of Nationalism and reconstruction in Sub-Saharan Africa

Nationalism is a composite phenomenon; it is, on the one hand, an ideological perspective and on the other hand a political one that affects various aspects of life: political, cultural and socio-economic. It is "...a political or social philosophy in which the welfare of the nation-state as an entity is considered paramount. Nationalism is basically a collective state of mind or consciousness in which people believe their primary duty and loyalty is to the nation-state" ("Nationalism").

According to this definition, Nationalism as a politico-social philosophy is about national identities through which nationalists identify themselves and act on behalf of a social group. It is therefore supported by a sense of relationship and/or kinship, based on a collective state of mind or consciousness, on the glorification of national virtues, and on resistance. These have been intrepid factors in most forms of Nationalism, as Ernest Gellner has outlined: "Nationalist sentiment is the feeling of anger aroused by the violation of the principle, or the feeling of satisfaction aroused by its fulfilment. A nationalist movement is one actuated by a sentiment of this kind." (1).

Gellner, here, views nationalist sentiments as phenomena that can be enthused by two principal factors: "the feeling of anger aroused by the violation of the principle, or the feeling of satisfaction aroused by its fulfilment." In other words, it is based on resistance and glorification respectively. The first factor is essential to modern African Nationalism, because it is linked to the historical relationship between Africa and the outside world, especially the West. First of all, the role played by the Trans-Saharan and Trans-Atlantic slave trades has been a formative factor of Nationalism in Sub-Saharan Africa. European colonisation, which subsequently replaced the Saharan and Atlantic slave trades, placed Africans under total domination by force, provoking and strengthening more nationalist sentiments in Africa.

Nationalism is extremely important in forming bonds to bind a social group together; it complements the official establishments of

11

society in delivering much of the cohesiveness and order essential for its wellbeing or for reconstruction.

Determining factors for the effective expression of Nationalism are the possession of a common history, religion, language or race. In other words the people concerned have to form a group and have to have something in common to identify themselves with as belonging to a nation. These factors motivate people to glorify their national identities; and the existence of a common identity and a formal authority structure over a large territory makes Nationalism a possibility. Some forms of Nationalism, the French Revolution for example, manifest a notion of popular sovereignty, and some observers might be tempted to consider Nationalism as possible only under a state of democracy. The form of Nationalism manifested in Germany characterising the German Empire and later Nazi Germany would belie this notion. François Mitterrand who had all along been haunted by the memories of World War II, stated in his last speech as President on European construction and the dangers of Nationalism, especially the Nazi version, before the European Parliament on 17 January 1995 that "Nationalism is war." President Mitterrand found European integration, which could be seen as a more collective form of Nationalism, as a means to promote a lasting peace. The sources and forms of Nationalism depend therefore on the particular history of the nation concerned.

Nationalism thus has a range of meanings, but its general concept basically encompasses two phenomena. Firstly it refers to the attitude of a people towards their nation, to glorify national identity and/or demonstrate national supremacy. Secondly it refers to the action taken by a people in seeking either to attain or preserve their independence or self-determination. It is this second sense that primarily concerns us most in trying to link Nationalism to reconstruction in Sub-Saharan Africa; because it aims at the acquisition and preservation of national independence, and subsequently specifically redressing the damages caused by the institutions of slavery, Colonialism and apartheid, and then the promotion of socio-economic development in general.

The contemporary international political system was born at the Treaty of Westphalia[6] in 1648, at a time when nations in Sub-Saharan

---

[6]Treaty of Westphalia; October 24, 1648 was the Peace Treaty between the Holy Roman Emperor and the King of France and their respective allies. The deliberations began in 1644 and ended in 1648 with two assemblies that produced the treaty

Africa were neither conceived as relevant States nor were Africans regarded as capable of sitting amongst the Western colonial powers; consequently Africans were excluded from the State building process. State formation, in pre-colonial Africa was however similar to that in most parts of the world, especially in Europe.[7] However the African process that similarly reflected confrontations between classes or communities to create larger administrative and political units was almost totally mired by European colonisation in Africa, leading to the imposition of foreign institutions, social relations and values.

The context of African Nationalism with regards to slavery and Colonialism, or even Imperialism vis-à-vis self-determination refers therefore to the struggle for full statehood with complete authority over the nations' affairs, both domestically and internationally. However the first concept of Nationalism is important as well, because Nationalism, as we have seen, can rarely be explained without a clear notion of the term 'nation'.

To further clarify the notion of Nationalism then, we must examine two concepts of primary importance: the nation and the State or country. Nationalism makes precise distinctions between the nation, which is a social (cultural and/or ethnic) group, and the State, which is a sovereign political entity in the form of a government ruling over one or more nations. This distinction further helps us to differentiate between the term Nationalism as affection or devotion to one's people, culture or ethnic group, and patriotism as love of one's State. This is essential because most actions or arguments are patriotic attempts to guarantee the survival of a particular State. The

---

between Spain and the Dutch (signed on January 30) and another between Emperor Ferdinand III, the other German princes, France, and Sweden (signed October 24). Territorial changes gave Sweden control of the Baltic Sea, ensured France a firm frontier west of the Rhine river, and provided their allies with additional lands. The Treaty confirmed independence for the United Provinces of the Netherlands and for the Swiss Confederation. It also confirmed the Peace of Augsburg and extended the religious toleration of Lutherans to include toleration of the Reformed (Calvinist) Church. The Holy Roman Empire was forced to recognize its German princes as absolute sovereigns in their own dominions, which greatly weakened its central authority.

[7]In most other parts of the world, State formation was a result of class conflicts, and in Europe in particular, in which early liberals denounced the "divine rights" of kings to rule.

State as a political institution has its own interests, and it derives and measures its power from the number of social groups it is able to control and levy taxes on. This means that the State and the nation have a conflict of interests. Often, States or outside forces do suppress nationalistic feelings and dismantle national groups in order to acquire, safeguard and consolidate their authority. Thus the key to understanding Nationalism is to comprehend the meaning of the word 'nation'. Contrary to the everyday use of the word, which customarily includes the different ethnic groups existing in the State, the nationalist concept of nation is based on the notion that people believe they belong to one social group bound by blood, language, religion, culture or other factors, just as Walker Conner qualifies the essence of the nation as "…a psychological bond that joins a people and differentiates it, in the subconscious convictions of its members, from all non-members in a most vital way …." (197). Therefore, contrary to most pedagogic analysis of Nationalism, nationalistic outlooks are based on the sense of sharing the same blood or language, and for Conner, national identity or bond is basically geared towards "lineage before language, history and other characteristics" (Ibid). Many States can therefore be considered as nations to some degree, but nations are mostly not sovereign in the strict sense. For example, the Casamance region of Senegal can be considered more as a nation than a State, because it does not possess sovereign authority, in an administrative sense, over its domestic and external affairs. If Casamance strives to acquire its sovereignty in an effort to maintain its cultural identity and establish its own political authority as a people, they would be demonstrating Nationalism. Indeed, some groups in Casamance are considered by the Senegalese government as rebels to the Senegalese State, and are manifesting a form of Nationalism in this respect. Another example of this phenomenon is the position of Corsica in France.

Reconstruction and/or development can equally take different forms and be interpreted differently depending on the context and the society in question. However, the common denominator of all forms of development is that each society or social group fights against diseases, insecurity and other dangers inherent to its existence. Humans thus struggle for food security, as well as protection against atmospheric uncertainties and danger, as a means of rendering their survival normal and safe. This struggle has forced humans to form groups, and create contact with other social groups. "...the term 'development' "...refers to the modalities of evolution and progress in all activities carried out by humans..." (Hulse 21) Development is therefore a natural and universal process of struggle for survival and protection by humans, although some social groups use force and other means to dominate, take advantage of and/or control other groups during the course of the process. Development should therefore be employed in a global perspective, since all societies or social groups have been engaged in the process of protecting themselves and improving their living conditions by creating socio-economic structures, systems and appropriate tools, although with natural differential acceleration. It is therefore only the levels of growth that differ from one society to another, and the main reason for the difference is socio-economic, which contains both economic and cultural aspects. The economic aspect of development is characterised by creativity and the invention of equipment for the production of goods and services for the economy of the society, in the agriculture and the manufacturing and service industries, which in turn contribute to increase productivity.

If there is a universal involvement of all and a natural progression in the process of development, what has gone wrong with the process in Africa? Why has Africa stagnated?

These questions refer us to the term underdevelopment, which does not mean the lack of socio-economic progress, because we have underlined that each nation has been engaged in a gradually evolving process of development. The socio-economic sense of underdevelopment refers to the state in which resources of a social group that generate growth are not used to their fullest potential, or are diverted to use in domains that are not strategic or productive to the economy in question, resulting in the process of progress becoming relatively slow.

Underdevelopment usually results from a combination of internal and external factors that allow the societies concerned to realise stagnation or just mere progression.

Africa is one of the richest regions of the world in terms of natural resources, yet it is also considered the poorest region in spite of this natural wealth. Some Western observers even consider as "apocalyptic" the overall situation of independent Africa. Bernard Lugan qualifies Sub-Saharan Africa as "fourth world"[8] where three decades of international aid was wasted; according to him, the failure is general. (Lugan 3).

In his book entitled, *How Europe Underdeveloped Africa*, Walter Rodney associated the underdevelopment of Africa with slavery and Imperialism and not a natural causality independent of voluntary intervention. According to Rodney, the slave trade served as an engine of the forced emigration of millions of Africans for several centuries. (105) The socio-economic impact of this human trading in Africa, which continues to be the subject of debate among historians, and according to some commentators, continues to affect Africa's reconstruction and development programme. In the same work Rodney defined development as:

> ... a many-sided process. At the level of the individual, it implies increased skill and capacity, greater freedom, creativity, self-discipline, responsibility and well-being. Some of these are virtual moral categories and are difficult to evaluate - depending as they do on the age in which one lives, one's class origins, and one's personal code of what is wrong. However, what is indispensable is that the achievement of any of those aspects of personal development is very much tied in with the state of the society as a whole. From earlier times, man found it convenient and necessary to come together in groups to hunt and for the sake of survival. The relations which develop within any given social group are crucial to an understanding of the society as a whole. Freedom, responsibility, skill, have real meaning only in terms of the relations of men in society (3).

Rodney here links liberty and creativity to development. To place the individual at the centre of the process of development therefore refers us to freedom, creativity, progress and material well-being, all in the context of the economy, the polity and culture. A society that is free is a society, according to these socio-cultural aspects, that effectively engages in creativity, which is one of the main keys to sustainable socio-economic progress. A free society is one which is able to produce more material goods and develop its cultures, to become richer. Freedom and creativity are therefore at the centre of all processes of development in a perfect competition, which make a comparative scale of local productivity. Development therefore recalls the freedom of the society concerned, which, in the context of Sub-Saharan Africa directly calls to mind slavery, Colonialism and

---

[8] Quart-monde.

apartheid and even the post-colonial relations between Africa and the outside world, notably the West, whose consequences are still present in this part of the continent both materially and morally. This is the reason behind our usage of the term reconstruction[9] to evoke the rectification of the interruption of the natural processes of development in Sub-Saharan Africa, just as the Second World War affected the process of development in some countries in Europe and Asia, even if the manner and duration of the two interruptions were not the same. The difference is that the dislocation of the African socio-political systems and structures lasted for at least three centuries, from the beginning of human kidnapping and trafficking in the 15th century, through Colonialism, and apartheid in South Africa, which only ended at the end of the 20th century, in the 1990s ; and even after the formal end of these phenomena, Africa's relationship with the international community, notably the West in this era of post-colonialism has been considered as not being based on genuine partnership in any of the domains.

For development or reconstruction to be effective, it has to be appropriate and sustainable. It must not be imposed from the outside and must also be effectively managed by the people concerned. It must meet the needs of the present generation without compromising those of future generations. The concept of development or reconstruction we are concerned with in this work is therefore "sustainable development." The formal roots of this concept can be traced back as early as the 18th century, to Mary Wollstonecraft's work, *A Vindication of the Rights of Women*, and especially Thomas Paine's *Rights of Man*, both appearing in 1792. These authors were concerned with empowering people over their own lives, to live according to their aspirations and values, instead of oppressing and/or colonising them. Sustainable development therefore serves as an important concept and bridge between the historical relationship of Africa and the outside world, notably the West.

The Brundtland Commission[10] outlined what has become the most quoted definition of sustainable development. This concept is

---

[9] Reconstruction and development are interchangeably used in this work.

[10] The Brundtland Commission, formally the World Commission on Environment and Development (WCED), named after its Chair Gro Harlem Brundtland, was convened by the United Nations in 1983. The commission was assigned to address

what has been considered as appropriate reconstruction for Africa through the primary participation of Africans themselves. The practical concept of African reconstruction in this work therefore refers to appropriate, effective and sustainable efforts to heal the wounds of Africa caused by our three historical phenomena. It refers to a process initiated, engineered, promoted and controlled by Africans themselves, with the genuine participation of the countries or social groups that played a role in the three phenomena in question.

---

growing concern "about the accelerating deterioration of the human environment and natural resources and the consequences of that deterioration for economic and social development." The Brundtland Commission defines sustainable development as "…development that meets the needs of the present without compromising the ability of future generations to meet their own needs."

Nationalism in West Africa: Pan-Africanism and Negritude.

The period between the two world conflicts was fundamental to Africa's struggle against European colonisation in a nationalistic perspective, because it awakened and reanimated its conscience. The birth of effective modern African Nationalism was therefore partly the consequence of European colonisation in Africa. A. Adu Boahen, in his work, *Topics in West African History*, defines African Nationalism as:

...the consciousness, on the part of individuals or groups of Africans, of membership of a nation-state either already existing or to which they aspire, and of a desire to achieve political and economic freedom, overall social and economic development as well as the cultural revival of that nation-state. (147)

This definition gives a global sense of modern African Nationalism as the aspiration and desire of Africans to obtain "political and economic freedom" as well as "overall social and cultural revival."

If Africans had not been effectively capable of changing their state of relegation in all the domains of life generated by the slave trades and European colonisation, the two world wars and the obligatory participation of African soldiers in both wars progressively demolished the notion of invulnerability that Sub-Saharan Africa had for the European colonisers. Modern nationalist movements reanimated by the Atlantic Charter,[11] however, concretely emerged

---

[11] The Atlantic Charter was the joint declaration issued on August 14, 1941, by the British Prime Minister, Winston Churchill and the American President, Franklin Delano Roosevelt. It was the outcome of the Atlantic Conference that took place in great secrecy aboard the U.S. heavy cruiser USS Augusta and the British battle cruiser HMS Prince of Wales. The two leaders and their staff discussed the general strategy of the war against the Axis Powers. The Atlantic Charter was the blueprint for the world after World War II, and is the basis of many of the international treaties and organizations that currently shape the world, including the United Nations Organisation and the General Agreement on Tariffs and Trade (GATT). Among the statements made in this propaganda manifesto, signed when the U.S. had not yet entered the war, were that neither the U.S. nor Britain sought aggrandisement and that both advocated the restoration of self-government to peoples forcibly deprived of it. It therefore became the basis of the independent movement after the war. The Atlantic Charter also contributed to the "changing of the guard" as the world's

only after World War II. During the two wars, especially the second one, there were contacts by African soldiers with all the peoples of the world in the struggle to liberate their own colonial masters from the hands of Nazi Germany. France and the United Kingdom took many of their conscripts from their colonies in Africa, including West Africa, to help fight against the Nazis; these involuntary soldiers had the same experience in Burma. But during the war the military capacity of the soldiers of the all-powerful Europe was questioned by African soldiers, who only had improvised training.

Modern African Nationalism was therefore strengthened by the participation of African soldiers in World War II, throwing light on the claim of superiority of the colonial masters. The "highly superior," civilised and powerful men fought one another, while the inferior "primitive savages" forcefully helped the one against the other. World War II therefore helped the plight of the African by shedding light on European pretensions and nationalistically pushing him towards the struggle for his own liberation and independence. In their African colonies, the Western Allies themselves promoted the idea of freedom in an attempt to gain support for their war effort. This gave African soldiers high expectations of freedom as compensation for their sacrifices in the war. But African soldiers had, in their participation in combat against Nazism and Fascism rediscovered their own identity in the process. The sentiment of fear and respect that they had envisioned for the European disappeared gradually during and after the war, leaving room for criticisms and action for their own deliverance.

The traditional Western concept of Nationalism was basically civic because it put the nation at the centre of interest. Nationalism in Germany and Italy, for example, were based on the notion of the supremacy of the nation's sovereignty. The nation-state attained its mature status in Europe during the 1800s, a period in which Nationalism noticeably became the principal foundation of Western civilisation. The various socio-political revolutions in England, France and the United States of America have demonstrated this phenomenon. The Glorious Revolution in England (1688), *la Révolution française* (1789-1799), and the American Civil War(1861-1865) paved the way for the modern nation-state.

---

leading power from Britain to the United States of America.

In colonial Africa Nationalism was altogether a different thing. After Europe's Scramble for Africa at the Berlin Conference of 1884-1885, the nations artificially created by this Conference according to the individual interests of the European countries that participated in it, did not show any phenomenon of civic and/or cultural identity as it had been known in Europe. The Berlin Conference and the partition of Africa by the European powers that followed it had two major impacts on African sovereignty and development. Firstly, it arbitrarily constituted territories and merged different social groups who traditionally had nothing in common and tore apart those that had almost everything in common. Secondly it forcefully implanted European economic and political structures into Africa, thereby attributing the continent a subordinate role in international relations primarily controlled by the West.

Most social groupings in Sub-Saharan Africa that had experienced cultural identity were separated after the Scramble, finding themselves gathered with others who were culturally different. These differences were, however, compellingly put aside by Africans because different groups found themselves governed by force by a single colonial master. The situation in Senegambia is an example of this phenomenon. In The Gambia tribal groups having completely different cultures, like the Mandingoes, the Wolofs, the Jolas, the Fullas and the Sarahules, found themselves under the same central colonial administration. The Mandingoes of Senegal and the Mandingoes of The Gambia had shared similar cultures, even if they had been ruled in different kingdoms. These almost united people were subsequently disconnected by the United Kingdom and France. Martin Meredith, in his work *The State of Africa* highlighted this phenomenon:

> African societies were rent apart: the Bakongo were partitioned between French Congo, Belgian Congo and Portuguese Angola; Somaliland was carved up between Britain, Italy and France. In all, the new boundaries cut through some 190 culture groups... Europe's new colonial territories enclosed hundreds of diverse and independent groups, with no common history, culture, language or religion. Nigeria, for example, contained as many as 205 ethno-linguistic groups. Officials sent to the Belgian Congo eventually identified six thousand chiefdoms there. (1-2)

To effectively stand against European colonisation these people in their struggles had to put aside the notion of pure culture as the basis of their struggle and lean on new identities: geographic, domination and exploitation. It is this reason that makes the notion of Nationalism in an African context different from the European notion of Nationalism. Of course African nationalists struggled for their nations in the same way as European nationalists, but the lack of strong cultural uniqueness obliged them to take up the identity that was common to all, domination and oppression, and promoted the notion of "Africanity." Also each coloniser imposed its culture by means of education, and the majority of the States arbitrarily created by European colonisers went through cultural transformations. Consequently, the Mandingoes in The Gambia and those in Senegal now behave completely differently; the Fulas in Nigeria and those in Cameroon as well. In spite of these differences they had a common identity, which, as we have pointed out, was no longer purely cultural: they had all undergone Western colonial oppression and exploitation.

Nationalism in colonial and post-colonial Africa was thus based on resistance to colonial domination and Imperialism. The whole of Africa had been invaded, partitioned and colonised, except Ethiopia and Liberia,[12] therefore it was the whole of Africa that was struggling. Some African leaders like Kwame Nkrumah had a strong awareness of this almost compulsory collective solidarity and responsibility to a point that he advocated during the Independence anniversary of Ghana in 1957, that there remained the need: "...to re-dedicate ourselves in the struggle to emancipate other countries in Africa... For our independence is meaningless unless it is linked up with the total liberation of the African continent." (*I speak of Freedom* 107).

Here Nkrumah was undoubtedly emphasising the notion of collective solidarity and responsibility as well as indicating the next phases of the struggle in a global perspective. This drives us to consider African Nationalism as any collective and organised form of resistance and efforts by Africans to regain and/or preserve African

---

[12] Ethiopia and Liberia were never colonised. The American Colonisation Society bought land in Liberia to settle free slaves but white rule had never existed there, and the majority of the population, about 95%, were native Africans; even though the freed slaves had been the ruling class for a long time. For Ethiopia, there was only a five year occupation by Italy, and the Italians never had a moment's peace during this occupation.

sovereignty in all domains of life and subsequently glorify African values.

There were early movements of Nationalism in Africa such as the Aborigines' Rights Protection Society in the Gold Coast (1897), the National Congress of South Africa (1912), and the National Congress of West Africa (1920). The conscience of West Africans, as far as Nationalism was concerned, had been effectively awakened by many factors including, as we have already noted, the participation of African soldiers, especially in World War II. The Atlantic Charter was strategically drawn up to help free the colonial masters from the hands of Nazi Germany, but with American strategic political insistence on decolonisation, also played a part. Anti-colonial struggles had taken many forms and nationalistic aspirations came from outside Africa as well. African students in Europe and especially the United States of America, notably Kwame Nkrumah of Ghana and Nnamdi Azikiwe of Nigeria, were the principal proponents of modern ideological struggles against colonisation and racism, especially in the period between the two wars. Several youth organisations also contributed to the struggle.[13] Newspapers such as the Negro World of Marcus Garvey and periodicals coming from outside Africa helped diffuse anti-racist and anti-colonial sentiments.[14] African branches of Marcus Garvey's Universal Improvement Association (UNIA) founded by Garvey himself in the United States of America in 1914 also inspired the expression of Nationalism in Africa.[15]

The term Negritude was coined by the Martinican poet and politician, Aimé Fernand David Césaire (1913–2008), for the first time in 1939 in his poem: *Return to My Native Land*.[16] This was a decisive step in the ideological struggle against racism, even if Césaire's doctrine was only elaborated after World War II. Pan-

---

[13]The Gold Coast Youth Conference, the Lagos Youth Movement, later renamed the Nigeria Youth Movement, the National Congress of British West Africa, the West Africa Students Union.

[14]The Lagos Weekly Record, the Lagos Daily News, the Gold Coast Times, in the late 19th and early 20th centuries.

[15]For example, the Nigeria Improvement Association founded in 1920 was an African branch of Marcus Garvey's association.

[16]*Le cahier d'un retour au pays natal.*

Africanism had already taken root and become the pivot of the struggle for freedom, principally in English West Africa. The two expressions became strategic in the struggle against Colonialism and racism, but they differed enormously in their characters, even if they seemed to have somewhat similar objectives.

The two movements that West Africans later used as political, philosophical and cultural weapons in their struggle against European Imperialism had their roots in the Americas and Europe. Pan-Africanism and Negritude as forms of Nationalism were therefore ideologies imported to West Africa respectively, to Ghana and Senegal specifically. These countries were under the domination of different colonial powers with completely different systems of administration. A comparative study of the two terms, relating each to post-Colonialism in Africa is necessary for a better understanding of their role in African reconstruction. To effectively analyse how the Anglophone and Francophone worlds in West Africa reacted politically and ideologically to Imperialism, it is necessary to take into account the personalities of the two protagonists of modern Nationalism in Anglophone and Francophone West Africa, namely Kwame Nkrumah of Ghana for Pan-Africanism and Léopold Sédar Senghor of Senegal for Negritude.

Pan-Africanism and Negritude might be running a similar course, but they were two different ideologies and adopted different approaches. At this juncture it is important to seek a working definition of each of the two movements we consider to be the main components of West African Nationalism.

At the third annual conference of the American Society of African Culture held in June 1960 at the University of Pennsylvania, the Senegalese founder of *Présence Africaine*, Alioune Diop, considered Pan-Africanism more or less the same as the concept of "African personality" or "Negritude." For the Black American historian, Rayford Logan, the objective of Pan-Africanism was to promote "self-government" by African countries south of the Sahara. The Nigerian journalist and politician Anthony Enahoro, at the same conference, provided a more expansive notion of Pan-Africanism, by considering it "a search for the economic, social, and cultural development of the continent," to avoid conflict amongst African States, and to promote African unity and influence in world affairs (Esebede 2). This meeting took place just three years before the inception of the OAU, and three years after the independence of Ghana.

The British journalist and writer Colin Legun provided a rather instinctive concept of Pan-Africanism as "essentially a movement of ideas and emotions; at times it achieves a synthesis, at times it remains at the level of antithesis"(14). J. Ayodele Langley, in his book, *Pan-Africanism and Nationalism in West Africa, 1900-1945: A Study in Ideology and Social Classes*, considers Pan-Africanism as a protest, "a refusal, a demand, and a utopia born of centuries of contact with Europe" (14). Ayodele's idea of protest or refusal is precise about the movement, but his description of Pan-Africanism as "a utopia" seemed rather specious, especially when Africans had already institutionalised the project of African unity since 1963.

The major ideas presented by these scholars of modern Pan-Africanism pointed out the African personality, solidarity amongst the people of African descent, African unity, and rehabilitation of Africa's lost pride, even if some analysts attempted to portray the movement as utopian. Most of the ideas reasonably fit the primary objectives of twentieth-century Pan-Africanism

Léopold Sédar Senghor, the co-founder of Negritude defined it as "...the set of cultural values such as expressed in life, institutions and works of Blacks"[17] (*Liberté 11, Négritude et Humanisme 9*).

This definition visibly detaches Negritude from the political sphere of Pan-Africanism. Manifestly then, the two terms are different in their nature, even if they seem to have similar objectives. Pan-Africanism therefore undertook a political struggle whilst Negritude chose cultural and literary trends. Africa and the African Diaspora through Pan-Africanism and Negritude attempted to affirm their common identity and destiny to serve as a link between them. Considering the concepts and manifestations by the protagonists of the two movements since 1900, we can formulate a comprehensive definition of Pan-Africanism and Negritude as political and cultural movements that seek to restore Africa's sovereignty and promote African integration and cooperation amongst the people of African descent, politically, economically and socially, while exalting African values with a sense of pride.

---

[17]*L'ensemble des valeurs culturelles du monde noir, telles qu'elles s'expriment dans la vie, les institutions et les œuvres des Noirs.*

The first formal expression of Pan-Africanism took place in London in 1900, when the idea was initiated by the Trinidadians, lawyer Sylvester Williams (1868–1911), and Georges Padmore (1902–1959). Subsequently Negritude was born in Paris amongst the francophone students. Despite its relative lack of political force, the aspirations of Negritude were welcome by the majority of Pan-Africanists, since it was built on the concept of cultural identity and a common destiny of black people.

What roles have Negritude and Pan-Africanism, under the umbrella of African Nationalism played in the struggle against Imperialism? If the goal of Nationalism was to free the African continent from the manacles of racism and Imperialism and to restore its sovereignty and dignity, how has this served post-colonial Africa in its process of sustainable socio-economic development as a form of repairing the damages caused by slavery, Colonialism and apartheid?

To answer these questions we have to explore the engagements of Pan-Africanism and Negritude in Africa's quest to regain its sovereignty, dignity and to integrate the continent. We will, by going along, note that African Nationalism has not only been based in West Africa, but the roots of effective anti-colonial struggle were situated precisely in this region, as we have noted in the role played by the Independence of Kwame Nkrumah's Ghana that liberated the former Gold Coast and subsequently contributed to the liberation of Sub-Saharan Africa as a whole. However South African Nationalism of the 20th century, and that led by Jomo Kenyatta and the Kikuyu in Kenya during colonisation have also played a major role in African liberation. South African Nationalism occupied a distinctive place through its battle against racial discrimination right into the late 1900s, although not purely leading an anti-imperial struggle.

The growth of Pan-Africanism

For the purpose of simplicity, we will divide the development of Pan-Africanism into three phases:

1. The first phase runs through the Trans-Saharan and Trans-Atlantic slave trades to the Independence of Ghana, shortly followed by the first Pan-African conference held on African soil in Accra, Ghana.[18]
2. The second phase, relatively shorter, corresponds to the period between the Independence of Ghana (1957) and the formation of the Organisation of African Unity (OAU) in 1963.
3. The third phase falls in the period of post-Independence in Africa, corresponding to the inception of the OAU and its subsequent transformation to the African Union in 2002.

It is important to situate the history of Pan-Africanism corresponding to its first phase in the Americas, before analysing the historical aspect proper to Africa, when Africans took the baton from their American counterparts, and applied it in an African context.

We have seen that Pan-Africanism has its roots in the Americas between the 19th and the 20th centuries, because the idea of uniting the peoples of Africa stemmed from the West Indies and the United States. Various groups of Africans quite separate in origin but united in their experience began to think of Africa as one idea and one land. All the former slaves knew that they were originally Africans, but almost none of them knew their country of origin, if they were Malians, Congolese, Senegalese, Nigerians, Gambians... Most of them viewed Africa as a huge continent of one bloc, without frontiers, in which all the black people lived together in harmony and fraternity. Late in the eighteenth century, when a separate Negro Church was established in Philadelphia in the United States, its founders called it "African." There were also various societies in the Diaspora,

---

[18] On April 15, 1958, in the city of Accra, Ghana, African leaders and political activists gathered at the first Conference of Independent African States. It was attended by representatives of the governments of Ethiopia, Ghana, Liberia, Libya, Morocco, Sudan, Tunisia, The United Arab Republic (which was the federation of Egypt and Syria) and representatives of the National Liberation Front of Algeria and the Union of the Peoples of Cameroon. This conference was significant in that it represented the first Pan-African Conference held on African soil. .

especially in the United States that called themselves "African." This was a reaction to the discrimination and exploitation generated by the slave trade. The African Diaspora that after the abolition of slavery continued to be the victim of racism, realised the need to come together in order to rehabilitate their African values and civilisation as a means of restoring the black man's personality and dignity. These ideas were not only developed in the United States of America, but also by the African Diaspora in other places in Latin America.

African slaves in the New World were excluded; they had been forcibly deported from Africa and reduced to the status of non-humans. Their dignity and personality were therefore confiscated from them, because their masters had been solely interested in their productive and reproductive capacities just like animals, rather than in their nature as humans. It was hard for most of these black slaves to cope with their position in their new societies. The Haitian revolution of 1791 and 1803, led by Toussaint Louverture[19] was an exemplary manifestation of resistance during the slave trade; it gave the black slaves a lot of hope and courage. Many, from this date, realised that freedom was possible, but that one had to work hard for it. The struggle against racism continued well after the slave trade, because the end of slavery did not put an end to inequality and the sufferings of the Negro.[20] The emancipation proclamation did not really free them simply because all its other domains of application after the formal ending of slavery remained theoretical.

---

[19] The Haitian Revolution (1791–1804) was the most successful African slave rebellion in the Western Hemisphere. It established Haiti as the first republic ruled by blacks. At the time of the revolution, Haiti was known as Saint-Domingue and was a colony of France. Through the revolution, people of African ancestry freed themselves from French slavery and colonisation. Although hundreds of rebellions occurred during the slave era, only the revolt on Saint-Domingue, beginning in 1791, succeeded in permanently liberating an entire island.

[20] The term "negro" means "black" in Portuguese and Spanish, which are derived from Latin and Greek. Negro was used in the English-speaking world to refer to a person of black appearance or ancestry. It does not matter whether this person was of African descent or not. The usage was accepted even by black people themselves, until the Civil Rights movement. However some African American leaders in the United States objected the term, preferring black, because the word Negro is associated with the long history of slavery, segregation and discrimination that treated African Americans as second class citizens, or even worse. It is now widely considered obsolete. Now the term African American is used on American citizens of black ancestry and black on the others.

At the end of World War I, American Negroes became more determined to obtain their rights. And in spite of being victims of racial discrimination, education progressively gave them the chance to travel, especially to Africa, and to emerge onto the international scene. They formed associations, created their own papers and made speeches that promoted the idea of a "common destiny" shared by black people all over the world. This idea was principally disseminated by Dr Edward W. Blyden and Bishop Alexander Walters of the African Episcopal Zion Church. These protagonists were inspired by an African of the Yoruba tribe, Majola Agbebi[21] of Lagos (Nigeria), who according to them represented the "African personality." On the occasion of the opening of the Liberian College in 1881, Dr Blyden warned Africans of the danger of losing their traditions by being assimilated by the West. "The African must advance by methods of his own…. We must show that we are able to go alone, to carve our own way." (Legun 529).

Booker Taliaferro Washington, considered by many African Americans as a man of exceptional personality was a leader in "promoting the interest" of black people in the United States of America. Around the end of the 19th century Booker T. Washington, born a slave in 1856, was the incontrovertible leader of the black community in the United States. He promoted the idea that intellectual training was worthless for black people, and the struggle for civil rights was illusive. B. T. Washington was said to have consequently attracted the attention of the American authorities to the point of obtaining funding for his project, the Professional Institute of Tuskegee, in Alabama where black people only received practical training, mostly manual, to become small agricultural farmers, carpenters, masons…, which according to some observers was appreciated by the government. Although Washington promoted the idea that intellectual culture could in no way serve black people, many people considered him as a model of African American struggle. However, in spite of his dominant position at that time, his ideas were assailed by William E. B. Du Bois who reproached him for his lack of interest in the right to vote, his antipathy towards higher education for black people and his general attitude that suggested

---

[21]Majola Agbebi had founded the first authentic African independent church in Nigeria, West Africa.

black people were responsible for their own condition. For this reason Du Bois considered him a partisan of white supremacy, an accusation that reduced him to an unconscious defender of the discriminatory ideology.

We have to reaffirm, going along, that this phase of the struggle of the African Diaspora against discrimination in the Americas was not Pan-Africanism in the proper sense of the word and in an African context.[22] When black intellectuals like George Padmore, William E.B. Du Bois and Marcus Garvey gave the struggle relatively more force, its ideas were later imported to Africa by Kwame Nkrumah of Ghana, Nnamdi Azikiwe of Nigeria and others, to later employ them in their fight for self- determination.

If at this primary stage of Pan-Africanism, the African Diaspora entirely united to fight against racism and promote the dignity and the cultural values of black Africans, they had different approaches and sometimes contrasting ideas about how to attain their objectives. Booker T Washington, we have seen, had refuted the idea of a struggle for civil rights and higher education for black people in the United States. William Du Bois rejected Washington's position and went on with the struggle for the right to vote and for higher education. Marcus Garvey's ideas were considered as the most radical amongst the pioneers of Pan-Africanism. Garvey was even considered by some as a "Moses" for black people, ready to lead them to the "promised land": Africa. With his ideas of "Black Zionism", Garvey was accused by some observers of inciting racial hatred and division. His self-motivated political philosophy was based on what Jean Paul Sartre qualified as "antiracist racism."[23]

It was in 1900 that a black Trinidadian barrister practising in London, Henry Sylvester-Williams, organised a "Pan-African" Conference in which some thirty delegates, mainly from England and the West Indies, and only a few Americans participated. This conference attracted attention, and the word "Pan-African" entered the English dictionary for the first time. The Conference was welcomed by the Lord Bishop of London, and through the efforts of Joseph Chamberlain,[24] Queen Victoria promised never to neglect the

---

[22]Most observers consider the movement at this level as Pan-Negroist, since it was championed by blacks in the Diaspora, principally fighting racial discrimination.

[23]*Racisme antiraciste.*

[24]Joseph Chamberlain was a British Member of Parliament from 1876 to 1914, and

welfare of "the native races." Pan-Africanism at the onset had therefore very little base in Sub-Saharan Africa, and the movement and its ideas remained dormant for a long time after the 1900 conference.

The Congress of Manchester held in 1945 marked the real phase of Pan-Africanism. The manifesto of this Congress proclaimed to "..affirm the right of all colonised peoples to control their own destiny. All colonies must be free from foreign imperialist control, whether political or economic" (pan-africanmovement.net). For the first time autonomy and independence were overtly pronounced for the African continent in the Pan-African movement, in other words the real force of Pan-Africanism had started to show itself. The 1950s were memorable years for the struggle for independence and autonomy when the first Pan-African conferences were organised on African soil by Kwame Nkrumah of Ghana and George Padmore.[25]

Before studying Pan-Africanism proper to West Africa, it is important to revisit the Pan-African inspiration in an American context, and its influence on Sub-Saharan Africa. We have advanced the idea that Pan-Negroism in the Americas before 1945 was a protest against racism and discrimination that brought together black people in the Diaspora. This in turn led them to demonstrate solidarity with the African continent to a point that they claimed autonomy and independence for all the African peoples. In the middle of the 20th century, Sub-Saharan Africa was almost totally occupied and colonised; accordingly Pan-Negroism had a greater influence on the lives of the people of Africa. After World War II, Africans started employing the ideas of Pan-Negroism in their struggle to liberate themselves. The black Diaspora in the United States of America contributed to the dissemination of Pan-Africanist ideologies thanks to the contacts between the two communities. All through the period of colonial domination in Africa, the links between the African-Americans and Sub-Saharan Africans was based on three important factors:

1.   Immigration and religion.

Colonial Secretary (controlling British colonies) from 1895 to 1903.

[25]The sixth congress in Kumasi in 1953 and the seventh congress in Accra in 1958, under the name of the First Conference of Black Peoples.

2. Education.
3. The political and economic situations of continental Africa.

Immigration of some black Americans to Africa, conceived spiritually as the "return", was an important factor. It was realised in two forms: firstly the emigration encouraged by the American Colonisation Society[26] during the first half of the 19th century, had incited African Americans to return to their "mother land" in order to restore their dignity. The movement of black Americans going back to settle in Africa also concerned the Caribbean Islands and Brazil. The second factor in this immigration was the coming of African American missionaries into Africa to introduce American evangelism. They made it possible for some Africans to go to the United States for further education, and this contributed very much to the development of Pan-Africanism in Africa. The missionaries present on African soil encouraged and even sponsored African students to go abroad for further education in mostly American institutions. Consequently many African students, especially from Anglophone West Africa, moved to the United States. During their studies, the students interacted with the black American community and participated in conferences and other educational and social activities. These contacts between the two black communities largely contributed to the political evolution of Africa especially in the colonial era. African students after their studies returned to their respective countries and encouraged others to enrol in mainly American institutions. The effect of the education received in America by African students was decisive on the political spectrum in colonial Africa, notably English West Africa. The writings of black Americans such as T Thomas Fortune, William B. Du Bois and the

---

[26]The American Colonisation Society was established in 1816 by Robert Finley as an attempt to satisfy two factions in the United States of America. Paradoxically, the two groups were on opposing sides regarding slavery in the early 1800s. The first group consisting of philanthropists, clergy and abolitionist wanted to free African slaves and their descendants and provide them with the prospect of returning to Africa. The second group were the slave owners who feared free people of colour and wanted to force them out of the United States. Both groups felt that free blacks would be unable to assimilate into the white society. John Randolph, a famous slave owner tagged free blacks "promoters of mischief." Henry Clay, a southern congressman and sympathiser with the plight of free blacks, believed that because of "unconquerable prejudice resulting from their colour, they never could amalgamate with the free whites."

ideologies of Marcus Garvey had great impact on the philosophies developed by African students in the United States.

The development of Pan-Africanism in West Africa was not only based on the contact between the African American community and Sub-Saharan Africa in the domain of emigration, education and religion. The political and economic situations in colonial Africa complemented it. After completing their studies, students returned to their countries naturally with the hope for a better life, as their education had changed their vision of the world. They had completely escaped colonial exploitation all through the years of their studies abroad. And even if their new societies away from their homes were submerged in racial discrimination, the two systems were not compatible, because the political situation in colonial Africa evoked total domination and exploitation. However the students returned home to find a colonial system more brutally manipulative and exploitative. With the idea of struggle for liberation and equality acquired during the years of their studies, it was normal that they changed their behaviour towards the colonisers and struggled for the liberation of their peoples.

The personalities behind the Pan-African movement in the Caribbean Islands and the United States all associated their Pan-African aspirations with the African continent. Since the formal commencement of Pan-Negroism in the 19th century, black people in the Caribbean Islands and the United States considered the African continent as a place to conciliate their sufferings, a place of awareness for the problems of the Diaspora: European and North American racism. After the first Pan-African conference, a multitude of meetings followed during which the militants formulated their petitions to the Society of Nations. At this initial stage, the intellectuals in the African Diaspora had three principal objectives:

i.   To combat racial discrimination against black people, especially in the West;
ii. to promote unity amongst black people all over the world;
iii. to obtain self-determination and Independence for Africa.

The third objective had less importance for the pioneers of the movement except maybe for Marcus Garvey. It was only after the 5th Pan-African congress in Manchester (UK) in 1945 that Kwame

Nkrumah attended with other African students, that Pan-Africanism started to become a real vehicle for anti-imperial struggle. It is this third objective that concerns us most, because it corresponded to the second phase of Pan-Africanism in a general perspective, but in proper terms, the first real phase as far as Sub-Saharan Africa was concerned. It was at this stage that the movement emerged and concentrated first on Anglophone West Africa to seriously serve the anti-colonial cause. At this moment, corresponding with the end of World War II, English West Africa, thanks to Pan-Africanism, went in search of itself. The link that existed between the black Americans and the African continent, particularly Anglophone West Africa was therefore one of the major catalysts of modern Pan-Africanism in Africa.

The shortcomings of post-colonial Nationalism: the O.A.U.

We have said that in its initial stage in Africa, Pan-Africanism was principally Anglophone West African; Francophone, Lusophone and Spanish speaking Africa participated very little in it. The absence of the subjects of Portuguese, Belgian and Spanish colonisers was not surprising, because they were practically denied the chance to go out of the colonies at least before World War II. However the absence of Francophone Africans was a bit unforeseen, because a good number of subjects of the French immigrated especially to Paris during the colonial era, where a Pan-African conference took place in 1919. However the different style of colonial administration of the British and the French most likely played a role in the initial absence of the French in Pan-Africanism, especially taking into account the French system of assimilation.

When Kwame Nkrumah and Nnamdi Azikiwe returned to their respective countries (Ghana and Nigeria) from the United States of America and Britain, the centre of gravity of Pan-Africanism shifted from the Diaspora to West Africa, in its theorisation as well as its localisation.

The most active rhetorician of Pan-Africanism in Africa became Kwame Nkrumah who effectively transformed it into a political movement mobilising the whole of Africa. Anglophone West Africa, precisely the Gold Coast (Ghana), was thus the initial base of modern Pan-Africanism in Africa. As soon as he returned to Ghana in 1947, Nkrumah reclaimed independence for his countrymen[27]. To everyone's surprise, especially imperial Britain itself, the Gold Coast imposed itself and became the country that mapped out the route for Sub-Saharan Africa's decolonisation, principally through the efforts of Nkrumah and his colleagues. He then, with his comrades, engineered the creation of an organisation for a political, economic and military union of African States, the institution of socialism in Africa, and the rehabilitation of the black man. The proclamation of Ghana's Independence on 6th March 1957 therefore changed the

---

[27] When Nkrumah returned to the Gold Coast, he joined the United Gold Coast Convention (UGCC). He subsequently broke with the UGCC to form the CPP, the political party that led him to victory.

centre of interest of Pan-Africanism to orientate it to the whole of Sub-Saharan Africa, thanks to the efforts of Kwame Nkrumah. This landmark date for Ghana's history was by the same token the landmark date for Nationalism in Sub-Saharan Africa. Nkrumah, who had exposed his ideas in a number of works, believed that only socialism could stop imperialist and capitalist exploitation in Africa, (*Africa Must Unite* 102).

We have seen that the first Pan-African conference of independent African states was organised by Kwame Nkrumah in the Ghanaian capital, Accra, in April 1958. It was followed by the All-African People's Conference in December the same year, and then by the inception of the Organisation of African Unity on May 25, 1963 in Addis Ababa, Ethiopia. The establishment of the OAU was therefore the revolutionary result of a series of regional Pan-African struggles and meetings. At this stage, the movement completely shifted from the African Diaspora that had pioneered it, to settle precisely in British West Africa.

However just like most socio-political movements at continental level, Pan-Africanism had not escaped the syndrome of controversies, division and rivalries. Divergence surfaced out of the movement just as it had existed between Booker T Washington and William B. Du Bois, who in turn had enormous difference with Marcus Garvey in its initial stage. The African leaders who led their countries to Independence[28] were all African nationalists. They all struggled for their country's sovereignty and Independence, but with different principles and methods.

Pan-Africanism was winning the battle against Imperialism, and it intensified the fight. When Ghana and most of Africa acquired their Independence, the idea of African integration became foremost, because now African nationalists did not have to directly confront Colonialism in the majority of Sub-Saharan African countries, even if there was the residual task of helping other countries that had yet to obtain their Independence.[29] The main task was to surmount other emerging problems, such as the encroachment of Imperialism in its larger context. There was a huge awareness and an urgent need for

---

[28] Kwame Nkrumah (Ghana), Julius Kambarage Nyerere (Tanganyika, unified with Zanzibar island to become Tanzania), Modibo Keïta (Mali), Sékou Touré (Guinea), Félix Houphouët-Boigny (Ivory Coast), Gamal Abdel Nasser (Egypt),

[29] The Portuguese colonies and a few French and English colonies.

unity and solidarity, but differences had already emerged between two principally divergent groups of African leaders with different philosophies about integration, even before the inception of the Organisation of African Unity. On the one hand, there was the Casablanca group, and the Monrovia group on the other. Those African countries with a more radical vision of the anti-imperial struggle in Africa adopted the Casablanca Charter in Morocco, on January 7, 1961.[30] On Kwame Nkrumah's initiatives, the Casablanca group, aligning their philosophy with that of the former Union of Soviet Socialist Republic, called on independent African countries to straight away embrace political, economic and military union. Other countries that formed the Monrovia group such as Nigeria and Liberia, later met in the Liberian capital, Monrovia, from May 8to 12, 1961, to propose a project of gradual economic unity that was considered by many observers as pro-Western. A few leaders of the remaining independent African states positioned themselves in-between. President Julius Nyerere of Tanzania figured in this group that recommended regional integration as a primary step towards the realisation of African unity. However these groups of African nationalist leaders of already independent African states[31] managed to partially put aside their differences to conceive the OAU. As soon as most countries in Africa obtained their Independence, statesmen from about thirty independent African countries met in the Ethiopian Capital, Addis Ababa to formally establish the OAU.

According to Article II of its Charter, the Organisation of African Unity had the following objectives:

i. To promote the unity and solidarity of the African States;
ii. to coordinate and intensify their cooperation and efforts to achieve a better life for the peoples of Africa;
iii. to defend their sovereignty, their territorial integrity and independence;
iv. to eradicate all forms of Colonialism from Africa; and
v. to promote international cooperation, having due regard to

---

[30] Nkrumah of Ghana, President Nasser of Egypt, Ahmed Sékou Touré of Guinea, were among the Heads of State who went in for that charter.

[31] Kwameh Nkrumah of Ghana, Tafawa Balewa of Nigéria, William Tolbert of Liberia, Julius Nyerere of Tanzanie, Ahmed Sékou Touré of Guinea, and the Emperor Haile Selassie of Ethiopia.

the Charter of the United Nations and the Universal Declaration of Human Rights.[32]

It could be noticed from the provisions of Article II of the Charter of the OAU that the Organisation was established to promote integration and solidarity amongst the African peoples. It also aimed at safeguarding the territorial integrity, sovereignty and independence of African States, by endeavouring to free the continent from all forms of Imperialism. This latter objective was, however, the most urgent. The organisation also aimed at promoting international co-operation, by giving serious consideration to the Charter of the United Nations and the Universal Declaration of Human Rights. The OAU also co-ordinated and harmonised the policies of its Member States in many domains.[33] When the Abuja Treaty that established the African Economic Community (AEC)[34]en tered into force in May 1994, the OAU started to operate on the basis of two legal instruments; from then on it was officially referred to as the OAU/AEC.

It is necessary to revisit the history of African Nationalism from the perspective of African Unity and reconstruction for a better concept of its successes and/or problems and especially its pertinence to the challenges that the continent had to face. Kwame Nkrumah had conceived Pan-Africanism as a movement that would completely liberate Africa and unite its peoples against all forms of Imperialism and marginalisation, the consequence of its dramatic encounters with the West. However since 1900 when the first Pan-African conference was organised by Henry Sylvester Williams in London, and after more than fifty years of the existence of the Organsiation of African Unity, African Nationalism was often scolded for not having obtained the desired results. Nationalism had effectively played a leading role in the liberation struggle of the African continent from Western colonisation in the formal sense, and indeed had contributed

---

[32] See the OAU Charter, Article II

[33] Political, diplomatic, economic, educational, cultural, health, welfare, scientific, technical and defence policies.

[34] The African Economic Community (AEC) is an organization of African Union Member States establishing grounds for mutual economic development among the majority of African states. The stated goals of the organization include the creation of free trade areas, customs union, a single market, a central bank, and a common currency thus establishing an economic and monetary union.

principally to killing apartheid in South Africa. But the same Nationalism was accused of failing to tackle the most pressing needs in post-colonial Africa: effective socio-economic development.

Since the creation of the OAU in 1963 up to its transformation to the AU, it had been the major symbol of the African reconstruction struggle and the promotion of African values. But it was accused of not having accomplished African integration in the economic and socio-cultural spheres which were the main reasons for its existence since the liberation of the African continent. This failure was symbolised by the transformation of the OAU to AU pronounced in July 2001 in Lusaka during its 37th and last summit. It is therefore essential to examine the factors behind the problems, especially in the perspective of African integration and reconstruction.

Many factors could be considered as responsible for this situation, amongst which the following were the most significant:

i. The Cold War;
ii. the radicalisation of Pan-Africanism and its affiliation to Marxist ideology;
iii. the controversy around the personality of Kwame Nkrumah;
iv. the conflict of colonial cultures in post-colonial Africa;
v. regionalism, tribalism and religious rivalry;
vi. politics and government; and
vii. the method of conflict management employed by the OAU in Africa.

Differences between African nationalists in their struggles that echoed differences amongst the protagonists of Pan-Negroism[35] were partly the consequence of the Cold War. This generated a division

---

[35] Some mulattos called Marcus Garvey"...a black gorilla..." and led a campaign against Garvey called "Garvey Must Go." W.E.B. Du Bois was a mulatto, who founded the integrationist organization NAACP. For Marcus the name of the NAACP shows that "Dubious" was a "pure coward" and not "pro Black" at all. Marcus considered Dubious as a bourgeoisie elitist who believed the struggle for black emancipation should be led by a so-called "talented tenth," and this bourgeoisie elitism according to Garvey was hypocritically in contradiction to his own Communist philosophy. Garvey also opposed Booker T. Washington who was the founder of the Tuskegee Institute.

between the two antagonist blocs in the world: the West led by the United States of America against the East, principally the Soviet Union; this division emerged at the beginning of the post-war period. The ideology of the Casablanca group, we have seen was revolutionary Pan-Africanism by its nature, simply because it was formulated on the principle of hard anti-imperial stance in Africa. It struggled to liberate Africa from all forms of Western Imperialism and tried to put an immediate end to the direct political domination that European Colonialism had imposed on Africa. The principal theorist of this version of Pan-Africanism was Kwame Nkrumah; he was also its most rigorous defender. This classic Pan-Africanism did not only aim at breaking the neck of Imperialism in Africa, it also had the objective of dismantling the geopolitical structure that the Berlin Conference had created in 1884. It was, for them, indispensable to bring together the peoples of Africa in a central government to completely get away from Imperialism and to become an active player in international relations and politics in the globalised world. Nkrumah's perspective was globally based on the idea that without this central government, independent Africa would remain on the margin of history. The Monrovia group on the other hand suggested gradual socio-economic ties as the basis of African integration. This difference was however temporarily and partially resolved on 25th May 1963 by the creation of the Organisation of African Unity, as we have seen.

The problems that faced the OAU were also engendered by the radicalisation of the movement that created division and sometimes contradictory ideas and principles. This was symbolised by the division of African leaders into two ideologically different camps well before the signing of the Charter of the OAU in Addis Ababa, as we have just seen.

Since the appearance of Marcus Garvey on the scene, Pan-Negroism had witnessed a radical phase, and this radicalism was manifestly imported to Anglophone West Africa by Kwame Nkrumah. Unlike the other founding fathers of the movement such as William B. Du Bois, Marcus Garvey was ready to fight all forms of racism and Imperialism "by any means necessary." He was not content with the simple pronouncement of ideologies and slogans. He managed to bring together people of African descent all over the world so as to obtain a decisive victory over Western Imperialism and racism. It was this radicalisation that partly generated intense divisions in the movement amongst its African protagonists even before the inception of the Organisation of African Unity. This was not totally negative, because it was considered a requirement for Africa to liberate itself. However it was crucial to post-colonial Nationalism in Africa, and in particular to the project of African Unity. Communist ideology that had been present in the movement since its creation intensified this radicalisation. Important personalities such as W.E.B. Du Bois,[36] Marc Kojo Tovalu Houénou and even George Padmore,[37] were all adept at Communism at least initially. When Nkrumah returned to Africa after his studies, he associated his version of Pan-Africanism with Communism.[38] Nkrumah once described himself as a "non-denominational Christian and a Marxian socialist," a combination that might have worried both the Communist East and the Christian West alike, but his strategies and ideologies leaned more towards Communism.

It was the political situation in colonial Africa that generated the force behind the classical Nationalism that Nkrumah pioneered. However, taking into account the post-colonial realities and the

---

[36] W.E. B. Du Bois was prosecuted by the Federal government in 1951, when he was 83 years old, for his affiliation with the Communist Party. A judge eventually threw out the case. Disillusioned with the United States, he officially joined the Communist Party in 1961 and moved to Ghana; he renounced his American citizenship more than a year later.

[37] George Padmore studied in Russia, but during his studies he had a disagreement with his Communist allies and broke ranks with them. He had disagreed about Russia's colonial policies. He came back to London where he re-launched his fight against Colonialism this time, not as a Communist. Padmore's switch away from Communism to Capitalism was very monumental, and re-shaped his political future thereafter. He then became very critical of other black Communist leaders, in particular African Marxists, and did not tolerate an affiliation of Pan-Africanism to Communism. He argued that Communism was just another form of European ideology that black people should ignore comprehensively like any other colonial ideology.

[38] Nkrumah more often employed the term Socialism, which is not very different from Communism. Socialism and Communism are alike in the sense that both systems of production are based on public ownership of the means of production and centralised planning. Socialism emerges directly out of Capitalism, as the first form of the new society. Communism is a further development or "higher stage" of Socialism.

atmosphere of the Cold War, most newly-independent States in Africa believed that their best interest lay in adopting a non-aligned position. Their economic conditions necessitated safeguarding cordial relations with their former colonial masters, but also with the other great powers. In spite of that, it was indispensable to fight hard against the colonisers leaning more on Socialism. The post-colonial era must therefore be different and for Nkrumah it was Socialism that would better serve the cause.

However, the adoption of Socialism or simply affiliating African Nationalism to the Soviet system was conflicting and paradoxical from pragmatic and patriotic points of view, because the struggle was principally against Imperialism. George Padmore reasonably expressed his Pan-African ideologies in his book *Pan-Africanism or Communism*, implying that the ideology of black Nationalism was incompatible with Communism. Padmore advanced the view that:

> Negroes are keenly aware that they are the most racially oppressed and economically exploited people in the world. They are also very much alive to the fact, demonstrated by the opportunistic and cynical behaviour of the Communists, that the latter's interest in them is dictated by the ever-changing tactics of Soviet foreign policy rather than by altruistic motives. Their politically minded intellectuals know that the oppressed Negro workers and peasants are regarded by the Communists as 'revolutionary expendables' in the global struggle of Communism against Western Capitalism. They know that Africans and people of African descent are courted primarily to tag on to the white proletariat, and thus to swell the 'revolutionary ranks' against the Imperialist enemies of the 'Soviet Fatherland.' This attitude towards the Negro is fundamentally part and parcel of the Communist philosophy relating to racial minorities and dependent peoples. (qtd. in Milne 134)

Nkrumah was said to be so disappointed by Padmore's criticism of Communism to the point of almost breaking rank with him politically. The association of the post-colonial struggle with Socialism obviously sent Africans back to another foreign system, a situation that symbolised escaping from one predator only to potentially throw oneself between the jaws of another, even if the relation or situation was relatively more ideological than exploitative. Africa consequently became an ideological battleground between the antagonist West and East, and this situation sent the continent into a new phase of Imperialism, however relatively less destructive it might be. During the Cold War the heroes of African liberation became advocates of either the Communist U.S.S.R. or the Capitalist West, affiliations that created tensions almost annihilating the cause of African integration and reconstruction.

Some observers might still argue that Africa benefited more from her adoption of Communist values, because the Soviet Union gave the continent the aid that it had not obtained from the West. If that idea cannot totally be refuted, it is important to note that no form of aid, especially from the two blocs and during the Cold War, was based on genuine assistance to promote socio-economic development in Africa as we have just seen in George Padmore's critique of Communist strategies in post-colonial Africa. Even the Marshal Plan had some strategic mission and vision. Be it the Soviet Union, the United States, France or the United Kingdom, aid has always strategically been attached to some strings on the feet of Africa, and its cost effects have been an enormous loss to its socio-economic values and principles, and created a self-fulfilling prophesy of African peoples lacking confidence in their own capacities and capabilities.

The two groups that emerged from this situation had conflicting ideologies and principles. The pro-Western Monrovia group held moderate views and strategies. It did not endorse the radical position of the Casablanca group that considered the call for immediate political and military union by Nkrumah and his colleagues, because it supposedly considered the position as an attempt by Nkrumah to become the supreme leader of the African continent. However, their own position sympathising with the West was neither an appropriate nor a practical solution to Africa's immediate post-colonial problems, because it represented one step backwards, after two steps forwards to liberating Africa.

Pan-Africanism could have continued its battle with a purely African formula that would enable it to walk slowly but surely away from Western Imperialism and not directly towards the Communist East, taking into account the political, and socio-economic realities of the new Africa and to incorporate in it appropriate democracy for Africa. We have indicated that the Casablanca and Monrovia groups however came to a temperate agreement in the end and instituted the Organisation of African Unity. The OAU was therefore initially more an organisation of compromise than a purely socio-political organisation with realistic projects.

This caused African Nationalism a lot of trouble, and difficulties in controlling the wheel of its vehicle. Even the Conference on Security, Stability Development and Co-operation in Africa (CSSDCA)[39] did not remedy the weakness. The OAU had difficulties putting an end to civil wars and military conflicts in Africa.

The controversy around the personality of Kwame Nkrumah also had an effect on Pan-Africanism. Nkrumah succeeded in what he himself called "the First Revolution," referring to the Independence of Ghana and thence the acceleration of the liberation of Sub-Saharan Africa from the manacles of Colonialism. However, he missed, or was made to miss the second revolution, which was the effective realisation of African unity and the construction of a modern independent African economy "based on Socialism" with the capacity to react politically on the international scene, which was the gist of Africa's quest for reconstruction. Between 1945 and 1947 Nkrumah made many trips to France and the United Kingdom in an attempt to draw support for his project of a Federation of Free West African States as a step towards African unity. When Nkrumah took power from the former colonial Britain and after his political victory, his opponents and other activists "incriminated" his engagements in the Pan-African movement. Most leaders believed that Nkrumah's actions were based on his personal interests, that his ambition was, in fact, to become the most important and powerful personality in Africa. Nkrumah's policies caused him and his vision for African unity a lot of trouble. His reputation grew amongst remarkable freedom fighters as he vociferously exposed the workings of neo-Colonialism in his writings and speeches. This increased reactionary forces against him, as exemplified by the feverish hostility to try to block the OAU meeting that was supposed to take place in Accra in 1965, because the achievement of the formation of a Union Government would be to the credit of Nkrumah. These charges directed towards Nkrumah in person therefore partially generated

---

[39] The Conference on Security, Stability Development and Co-operation in Africa (CSSDCA) was adopted at the 36th Session of the Assembly in Lomé, Togo on July 2000. It is a policy development process created to function within the framework of the African Union. It is one of two special programs of the African Union, (the other being the New Partnership for Africa's Development (NEPAD).

and aggravated the division amongst African nationalists, turning the glorious page of African struggle to a near failure.

Africa is composed of 55 recognised sovereign states, (Morocco included, which is not part of the African Union) with an estimated population in 2013 of 1.033 billion. (africacheck.org) In each of these States there are many ethnic groups, totaling several thousand different ethnic groups. In The Gambia principally we find the Mandingoes, the Wolofs, the Jolas, the Sereres, the Fulas, the Manjagoes, the Akus... In Nigeria there are the Yorubas, the Hausas, the Ibos, the Fulas... In Ghana, we find the Ashanti, the Fantes, the Nzimas,[40] the Baules..., In Sierra Leone there are the Temnes, the Mendes, the Creoles... In all these States each ethnic group possesses its own different culture, language and mode of life, but most tribes have a slightly common customary trend. However, the Mandingoes of The Gambia and those in Senegal now behave completely differently, and so too the Wolofs and the Fulas in the two countries. This is because the Mandingoes in The Gambia have adopted the British colonial culture and those in Senegal behave almost like the French who colonised them. Sub-Saharan Africans, before being colonised, had experienced cultural heterogeneity, resulting from the existence of different ethnic groups, but that was not as pronounced as now and they were living side by side in relative harmony. Colonial cultures appeared in Africa during colonisation, and had some negative impact on the African continent and its reconstruction efforts.

The presence of these different colonial cultures in Africa made the realisation of the project of African integration difficult, because of the different colonial acculturations of independent Sub-Saharan African States. There was a huge difference and even a sort of rivalry between Francophone Africa and Anglophone Africa even after independence, especially in the immediate post-colonial era. According to June Milne:

> Some of the Francophone states threatened not to attend the OAU Summit meeting to take place in Accra in October 1965, to sabotage the Conference. It proved impossible for Nkrumah to get sufficient votes in favour of his proposals for an Executive Council and an African High Command designed to transform the OAU into an

---

[40] A minority ethnic group to which Kwame Nkrumah belonged.

organisation with the necessary machinery to swiftly and effectively solve African problems. (101)

The confederation between Ghana, Guinea and Mali[41] is a striking example of this phenomenon. It was to unify Anglophone elite in Ghana, and Francophone elite in Guinea and Mali; Ghana had undergone a different colonial system from Guinea and Mali, hence the two camps using different modes of public administration, and different official languages, English and French. The collapse of the confederation between Anglophone Gambia and Francophone Senegal (1982-1989) also demonstrated, amongst other things, the frictions and difficulties posed by the two colonial cultures in Africa. This situation was aggravated by problems of infrastructure in many sectors especially in the communication sector.[42] In this now more heterogeneous and fragile atmosphere, African Nationalism will continue to face a tough battle as long as these colonial cultures are not kicked away.

Regionalism also played an important role in the problems of the OAU in post-colonial Africa. Frantz Fanon seemed to be the most perceptive on the subject, in spite of his Marxist ideas that some observers considered extremist. In his book entitled *The Wretched of the Earth*, he qualified the project of African unity as "vague formula, yet one to which the men and women of Africa were passionately attached, and whose operative value served to bring immense pressure to bear on Colonialism…" (116). He further argued that African Nationalism wasted its efforts in the struggle because it:

… takes off the mask, and crumbles into regionalism inside the hollow shell of nationality itself. The national bourgeoisie, since it is strung up to defend its immediate interests, and sees no farther than the end of its nose, reveals itself incapable of simply bringing national

---

[41]On 23 November 1958 a Ghana-Guinea Union was formed. In May 1959 it was renamed the Union of African States. In April 1961 Mali joined the Union; it disintegrated in 1962, when Guinea turned to the United States, against the Marxist idea of the other partners, who adopted the Soviet system, the main adversary of the United States during the Cold War.

[42]The projected regional integration between Tanzania, Kenya and Uganda, born in 1967, failed a decade later in a very tense atmosphere, especially between Tanzania and Uganda, despite the fact that these countries share not only the same colonial (official) language, English, but also the same African language, Kiswahili. Modibo Keita and Leopold Sedar Senghor tried a union of Mali and Senegal that also failed.

unity into being, or of building up the nation on a stable and productive basis. The national front which has forced Colonialism to withdraw cracks up, and wastes the victory it has gained.[43] (116-117)

According to Frantz Fanon then, the national awareness of Africans was full of contradictions and self-centredness, which had to be solved beforehand. Regionalism was a factor that contributed to retarding the project of African reconstruction, and was guarded by the different groups to protect their "immediate interests", generated by lack of vision for the future of the continent. Nationalism that had exercised extremely tough pressure on Imperialism to the point of nearly dismantling it later took off its uniform prematurely and largely faded away into the wilderness, mainly because of regionalism. Fanon accused the national or local bourgeoisie of being responsible for this state, for only attempting to secure their personal interests and the sovereignty of their respective nations after Independence, consequently becoming incapable of shouldering the project of continental integration.

Chenua Achebe, in his novel *Man of the People* wrote:

The trouble with our nation (...) was that none of us had been indoors long enough to be able to say "To hell with it." We had all been in the rain together until yesterday. Then a handful of us – the smart and the lucky and hardly ever the best – had scrambled for the one shelter our former rulers left, and had taken it over and barricaded themselves in. (37)

Achebe's argument representatively echoes Fanon's critiques that the national or local bourgeoisie of immediate post-colonial Africa had short-sightedly safeguarded their personal interests to the detriment of African reconstruction. Nationalism in the form of an African continental front had won the battle against Colonialism, but it then wasted its efforts, because the African bourgeoisie was engaged in quarrelsome projects, and national and regional egoism.

Religious rivalry and tribalism as well as politics and government in Africa also had a hand in post-colonial African reconstruction.

[43] *...dévoile son vrai visage et s'émiette en régionalismes à l'intérieur d'une même réalité nationale. La bourgeoisie nationale, par ce qu'elle est crispée sur ses intérêts immédiats, parce qu'elle ne voit pas plus loin que le bout de ses ongles, se révèle incapable de réaliser la simple unité nationale, incapable d'édifier la nation sur des bases solides et fécondes. Le front national qui avait fait reculer le Colonialisme se disloque et consume sa défaite.*

Religious rivalry was engineered in Sub-Saharan Africa, aggravated by the antipathy between Islam and Christianity. During colonisation, Christian missionaries recurrently exposed the idea that before European colonisation most African empires were dislocated by Arab invasions. They purported that Arab occupation paved the way for Western colonisation, and further tried to point out Arab Imperialism condemning it as cultural Imperialism by Islam on African societies.

African Nationalism had severely fought Colonialism and nearly exterminated it, but the latter regained its force under the umbrella of Imperialism and engineered tribalism, regionalism and spiritual rivalry to dismantle African endeavours. Africa of the immediate post-Independence era thence became incapable of countering the situation, and it became more divided, adversely hampering efforts. It divided the people of the continent further; one region of Africa against another region of the same Africa, countries against countries, and Christianity and Islam against each other. Colonialism this time appeared in the form of ideological and spiritual Imperialism, with the main objective of weakening and holding back the process of African reconstruction. A continental project of reconstruction based on the quest for integration, solidarity and socio-economic progress required competent, sincere, confident and especially autonomous actors with principles and self-discipline to turn it to a real machine to make appropriate decisions and embark on the right projects for the people.

Unity in any community is liable to the preconditions of total independence and peace, without which it is practically unattainable. Yet, immediate post-colonial Sub-Saharan Africa had been an extraordinary zone of political and civil conflicts, because of the factors we have just mentioned. History has taught us that peace and stability have not been lasting in post-colonial Africa, because conflict is ubiquitous on the continent especially in Sub-Saharan Africa. Reggae star from Ivory Coast, Alpha Blondy has pointed this out in one of his pieces entitled *It Hurts Me*:[44]

> When I think today that
> in Africa we destroy ourselves
> While the powers laugh
> they like to see us disunited oh!
> ....

---

[44] *Ça me fait mal.*

The hotbeds of tensions multiply
Orphans multiply
Arms multiply
Wars multiply
Deaths multiply
and our cries amplify
our misery amplifies
.... [45]

In this track, Mr Blondy expressed the futility and destructiveness of conflict to Africa's socio-economic recovery programme, because these wars generate death and misery, block socio-economic progress and strengthen disunity.

All through its history, the OAU succeeded in resolving some disputes, but concerning the prevention of conflict, maintaining lasting peace and the promotion of sustainable socio-economic development, it has not been totally successful. We have said that in an atmosphere of tension and conflict, it is practically impossible to exercise realistic socio-economic activities. To understand the method employed by the OAU in trying to resolve conflicts and maintain peace in Africa, an understanding of article III of its Charter, which concerned the principles stipulating the organisation's method of conflict management, is essential:

The Member States, in pursuit of the purposes stated in Article II solemnly affirm and declare their adherence to the following principles:

    i. The sovereign equality of all Member States;
   ii. non-interference in the internal affairs of States;

---

[45]*Quand je pense qu'aujourd'hui*
en Afrique on se détruit
tandis que les puissance rient
elles aiment nous voir désunis oh !!
...
Les foyers de tensions se multiplient
Les orphelins se multiplient
Les armes se multiplient
Les guerres se multiplient
Les morts se multiplient
et nos pleures s'amplifient
notre misère s'amplifie

iii. respect for the sovereignty and territorial integrity of each State and for its inalienable right to independent existence;

iv. peaceful settlement of disputes by negotiation, mediation, conciliation or arbitration;

v. unreserved condemnation, in all its forms, of political assassination as well as of subversive activities on the part of neighbouring States or any other States;

vi. absolute dedication to the total emancipation of the African territories which are still dependent;

vii. affirmation of a policy of non-alignment with regard to all blocs.

The first three principles: sovereign equality, non-interference and respect for sovereignty and territorial integrity, were obvious and logical reflections on the problems caused by Colonialism in Africa. The forth principle: peaceful settlement of disputes, corresponded to the idea of non-violence, peace and stability that the African leaders wanted to convey and promote.

The most obvious motivation behind "Non-interference in the internal affairs of States" was the logical desire of African leaders to safeguard their independence, to be left alone to choose their own trends of public administration and government and to embark on their own processes of development. Manifestly, this Charter was intended to caution the international community, especially the former colonial masters, that the OAU would not entertain any form of imperial encroachment. Consequently, and logically meaning that the caution did not concern Member States of the organisation collectively, because the OAU could not resolve conflicts effectively without intervening in the affairs of the States affected by the conflict in question. Therefore there had either been a misinterpretation of the article on "Non-interference…" or deliberate negligence of its provision on the pretext that it did not allow Member States to intervene in the domestic affairs of another Member State in order to put an end to a conflict. If the article stipulated that Member States must not interfere in the internal affairs of other Member States, it did not outright and reasonably prohibit the Member States of the OAU from collectively finding a solution, which comes to the same thing as interfering directly in the affairs of those countries at the centre of a conflict. The principle of the Charter can therefore be interpreted as only concerning those countries who were not members of the OAU.

Article III should have therefore been interpreted again in a way to make it effectively applicable taking into account Africa's political realities. The Organisation should have invented a mechanism of intervention in conflicts so as to manage them effectively. This mechanism should lead to the creation of a democratic culture of politics and government in Africa. The means to do that was not a question of case law, but that of common sense and pragmatic politics and government for conflict prevention to be effectively possible. It is important to elucidate principle vii of Article III concerning the policy of non-alignment with regard to all blocs of power. This was a reflection on the Cold War of East-West antagonism over government and administration. The OAU cautiously opted for non-alignment, but it was rather theoretical. One group of African leaders embraced the ideologies of the Communist East and the other group followed the ideas of the Capitalist West. This echoes Frantz Fanon's idea of African Nationalism being a vague formula, and Kwame's description of the Charter of the OAU as a Charter of intent instead of positive action.

We have also observed that most attempts at political integration had practically failed in post-colonial Africa. The Organisation of African Unity via its Liberation Committee endeavoured to liberate the continent, and to dismantle apartheid. It accomplished the two most pressing problems since Africa was formally liberated and apartheid was defeated in South Africain the early 1990s. However the formation of a commanding central government as a factor of effective reconstruction that had preoccupied Kwame Nkrumah and his compatriots remained a challenge symbolising some failure. The fact that the Organisation of African Unity continued to base its programmes on colonial cultures, and states created artificially at the Berlin Conference instead of creating a coherent Federation of African States, made reconstruction efforts neglect the realities on the continent. African nationalists and policy-makers must realise the necessity to restructure nation-states to completely kick away the negative effects of slavery and Colonialism. The reconstruction efforts require African countries to put aside some portions of their sovereignties. Failure to reform risks keeping the continent continuously bound to the heritage of Colonialism. The present African States could keep a part of their sovereignty and shed a part to an African central authority. It is also necessary that Member

51

States adopt purely African principles and values to guide the Organisation's efforts for reconstruction, in other words, Africa should lean on its own socio-cultural values.

The African Union: lessons and perspectives

The OAU was formed, as we have noted, as a compromise between revolutionary and moderate Pan-Africanism. In spite of this, it managed to partially heal Africa's wounds generated by the slave trade, Colonialism and apartheid, and to alleviate the continent's marginalisation on the international scene. It had also been a vector for Africa to consolidate its independence, and to have the capacity to stand on its own two feet.

It had become manifest since 1979, when the Organisation established the Committee on the Review of the Charter, that an amendment of the OAU Charter was needed in order to strengthen the Pan-African Organisation and prepare it more effectively for the challenges of this ever-globalised and changing world. This need for greater efficiency and effectiveness to combine the polity, the economy and culture as expressed in the Abuja Treaty[46], required urgent action. But in spite of various attempts and meetings the Charter Review Committee did not formulate substantive amendments. However the adoption of the Abuja Treaty by the majority of OAU Member States gave the idea of African unity new and more constructive directions. The treaty proposed the establishment of an African Economic Community to promote and safeguard economic integration on the continent. According to this proposition, the existence of the multiple Regional Economic Communities[47] justified the creation of a central African Economic Community.

---

[46] The Abuja Treaty is an international Pan-African agreement signed on June 3 1991 in Abuja, Nigeria. It created the African Economic Community. The African Central Bank (ACB) was one of the three financial institutions of the African Union that would take over responsibilities of the African Monetary Fund over time. The creation of the ACB, to be completed by 2028 was first agreed upon in the 1991 Abuja Treaty. The 1999Sirte called for a speeding up of this process with creation by 2020.

[47]The Economic Community of West African States (ECOWAS), the Arab Maghreb Union (AMU), the East African Community (EAC), the Economic Community of Central African States (ECCAS), the South African Development Community (SADC).

At the Extraordinary Summit of the OAU in Sirte, Libya on 9 September 1999, the transformation of the OAU to the African Union in conformity with the ultimate objectives of the OAU Charter and the provisions of the Treaty establishing the African Economic Community (AEC) was called for by the initiative of the late Libyan leader Muammar Al Gaddafi. Consequently the OAU and the AEC were now to be incorporated into one institution, the African Union. The Organisation of African Unity was then transformed into the African Union. The 2000 OAU/AEC Assembly of Heads of State and Government in the capital of Togo, Lomé, was held to adopt the Constitutive Act of the African Union, according to the Sirte Declaration of September 9, 1999. The decision that established the African Union was subsequently adopted by the Heads of State and Government at the 5th Extraordinary Summit held in Sirte, Libya on March 1 and 2, 2001. The legal requirements for the Union were completed when the 36th instrument of ratification of the Constitutive Act of the African Union was deposited. South Africa became the 35th member state to deposit the instrument of ratification of the Constitutive Act of the African Union on April 23, 2001 at the OAU General Secretariat. On April 26, 2001 Nigeria deposited its instrument of ratification, becoming the 36th Member State to ratify the Act. This concluded the two-thirds requirement and the Act entered into force on May 26, 2001, formally establishing a new Pan-African body exactly one month after its Constitutive Act was ratified. The Congress of Heads of State and Government that followed this ratification took place in Durban, South Africa in July 2002.

The African Union (AU) then replaced the Organisation of African Unity (OAU), after the latter's almost 40 years of existence. For most, especially African observers, the creation of the African Union comes with new hopes for the Pan-African dream for an African federal government with a common foreign policy, African currency, defence and closer economic ties and programmes. We have outlined that the OAU was only moderately successful, and the question now is: can the AU do any better?

To perceive the potential of the new African Union, it is necessary to make an ingenious comparison between the organs, structures and functioning of the OAU and the AU. The AU has envisaged the realisation of economic and political integration of the African continent, a project that the OAU had only partially considered and was not able to fully accomplish. The institutions of the new African Union should therefore reflect the historic experience of the OAU. In its Constitutive Act, the principles of the AU affirm amongst others:

i. Promotion of social justice to ensure balanced economic development;
ii. respect for the sanctity of human life, condemnation and rejection of impunity and political assassination, acts of terrorism and subversive activities;
iii. condemnation and rejection of unconstitutional changes of governments. (Article 4 n,o,p).

These were not present in the Charter of the OAU, meaning that the Constitutive Act of the AU is wider and more specific with regards to its objectives and principles. This difference is illustrated in Article 3, (g) and (h) of the Constitutive Act, which stipulate to "promote democratic principles and institutions, popular participation and good governance; promote and protect human and peoples' rights in accordance with the African Charter on Human and Peoples' Rights and other relevant human rights instruments."

The Constitutive Act of the AU contains several organs and institutions that were not in the Charter of the OAU. The most important are the Social and Economic Council (Article 22), the Pan-African Parliament (Article 17) and the African Court of Justice (Article 18). The transformation of the OAU to the AU therefore shows that the African peoples are not unaware of the gravity of the dangers surrounding the continent. The marginalisation that the continent has been victim of in the international politico-economic system has positioned Africa behind the other continents in almost all domains of life. The AU is therefore evidently driving Africa on a more constructive and pragmatic route to unity and reconstruction. For this to yield concrete and effective results and lead the new African Union to realise the project of integration that its predecessor started and only partly succeeded, it had to continue changing strategy, which seems to be the case now with the apprenticeship of pragmatism; even if some critics have judged that the objectives presented by the initiative of Muammar Al Gaddafi in Sirte in September 1999 are not radically different from the objectives formulated by the founders of the OAU in Addis Ababa in 1963.

This pragmatism, however, must not be based on the application of uncoordinated initiatives and tasks without concrete projects and actions as follow-up. The principal purpose is to promote sustainable socio-economic development, democracy and good governance, but by the initiative and self-control of Africans themselves. History has taught Africa that any ideological inventiveness coming from the outside has never totally been based on genuinely helping the continent out. The powers are thick on the ground safeguarding their institutions, their systems, their domination, and consolidating their efforts to marginalise the rest of the world especially the South. Africans cannot, in view of the nature of globalisation and international relations, avoid dealing with the rest of the world, but they should majorly operate on their own principles and have confidence in their own strategies and systems. In terms of democracy, African States should follow the footsteps of Ghana, Kenya, Senegal and Zambia in this new era of the African Renaissance, not only because these countries have changed their governments, but simply because their manifestation of relative democracy has been consummate, in almost all domains of government. After the death of President John Evans Atta Mills, on July 24, 2012, Ghana peacefully transferred power to Vice President John Mahama on July 25, 2012, a confirmation of the country's maturity and respect for the Constitution and democratic principles.

The African Union should take account of the fact that a State must be constitutionally very advanced for the leaders to quit power voluntarily according to their constitutions, and even some Western "democratic" States have been affected by this syndrome of leaders trying to hang on to power, especially if the constitutions do not limit terms in office. In the United Kingdom, Tony Blair was almost forced out of power by his Labour colleagues; and in France it was only Jacques Chirac's scepticism about the possibility of winning a third term that convinced him to stay out of the 2007 elections. Constitutions are no game-tools, and leaders should be democratically accountable to their people. The limitation of political mandate to a term constitutionally reasonable according to Africa's socio-political realities should be considered and encouraged by the African Union to become part of African political culture just as in the USA and some Western European countries. These democratic principles must not necessarily be a carbon copy of those in the West, because democracy is just like love in a family: it must come from within to be effective, and the people concerned must understand and accept it.

Article 4p of The Constitutive Act of the African Union has condemned and rejected "...unconstitutional changes of governments."[48] During the 7th Summit of the Heads of State and Government of the Member States of the African Union in Banjul, Gambia, between June 25 and July 2, 2006, intended for the adoption of the Charter for Democracy, the leaders, however, failed to adopt the Charter, because of disagreement on its terms. (Africa-union.org) The African Union must react to adopt some criteria to promote political socialism in order to inculcate a culture of democracy in the people, but this should be its own appropriate democracy based on African cultural values.

The inception of the African Union is considered and accepted by the people as a fresh beginning for Africans to regulate their own problems and take in their own hands the machine to transform their independence to an effective and sustainable one as a form of appropriate reconstruction. This is demonstrated by the African Union's evaluation of the procedure of conflict resolution, in Article 4 (g) and (h) of its Constitutive Act; "Non-interference by any Member State in the internal affairs of another" has been reproduced, but cautiously and pragmatically adjusted with another subsection (h) that affirms: "The right of the Union to intervene in a Member State pursuant to a decision of the Assembly in respect of grave circumstances, namely war crimes, genocide and crimes against humanity."

The role of external forces such as slavery and Colonialism are not insignificant, but it is about time that the African peoples learnt to walk on their own track towards reconstruction, integration and development. History might never forget nor forgive, but man can forgive, or at least, constructively pretend to forget; Africa cannot thereby judge history up to the end of time, with regards to slavery, Colonialism and apartheid.

The participation of the civil society, non-governmental organisation and professional associations in African reconstruction is requisite and must be encouraged more. The Cold War having ended, the African continent is now facing new threats of

[48] Article 4, P. This is not mentioned in the Charter of the OAU.

marginalisation, because Africa is now neither strategically important to the West nor to the East because the USSR is non-existent. Other partners are apparently doing positive business in Africa, but the continent should be more cautious even if these new partners actually attach no strings to her feet in their partnership. The West, especially the United States, has new priorities, in the Middle East and in the "War against Terror." Africa should therefore drive its own vehicle. Also, the strategy of the United Nations vis-à-vis world conflicts has transformed. The United Nations now adopt diplomacy to resolve conflicts in the world instead of direct confrontation, preferring regional organisations to play a major role in the resolution of conflicts that generate in their respective regions. For example to keep peace in Rwanda, the United Nations asked for an African peacekeeping force.

The controversy of Negritude?

The concept of Negritude, as we have learnt, was coined by Aimé Césaire while in conversation with his companions, Léopold Sédar Senghor from Senegal and Léon G. Damas from Guyana. Its ideology, however, has its roots in the thoughts of Dr Edward William Blyden, Martin Delany, and especially W.E.B. Du Bois' famous book *The Soul of the Black Folk* that tried to upgrade the black man, alongside accusing Booker T Washington's strategy of keeping the Negro down rather than liberating him.

These personalities made great efforts in their writings to erase the scars of slavery from black people. Aimé Césaire's invention of the term "Negritude" thus resulted from the inspiration he got from the Harlem Renaissance,[49] in which other writers like the Jamaican-born poet and novelist, Claude McKay and the African American Langston Hughes enunciated the richness of black culture. Léopold Sédar Senghor who adopted the term and was considered by many as the co-inventor of Negritude, described Claude McKay as "the true inventor of Negritude" (britannica.com). Negritude is therefore another form of Pan-Africanism tailored in the French style and centred on black culture and identity. It is therefore necessary to compare and contrast the two concepts with regards to the struggle against racism and Imperialism and in the perspective of African reconstruction.

We have seen that Césaire formally employed the term in writing for the first time in 1939 in his poem *The Return to the Native Land*:[50]

> My Negritude is not a stone, its deafness dashed against the clamour of the day my Negritude is not an opaque spot of dead water on the dead eye of the earth my Negritude is neither a tower nor a cathedral it plunges into the red flesh of the soil it plunges into the ardent flesh of the sky it pierces the opaque prostration with its upright patience (Césaire 46-47)[51]

---

[49] A literary and artistic movement that emerged among a group of black thinkers and artists in the United States, in New York City, during the 1920s. At the time, it was known as the "New Negro Movement," named after the 1925 anthology by Alain Locke.

[50] *Cahier d'un retour au pays natal.*

[51] *ma negritude n'est pas une pierre, sa surdite ruee contre*

This poem manifestly claims the "self-estrangement" that faced the black man both as a subject and an object, especially in the West. It shows that the estranged black identity is forced to confront itself as an object, which generates a process of self-awareness in him to struggle to break the bonds of subjugation. However, if in the poem Césaire presents the black man as an object, it is in no way a lifeless object like "stone" or "dead water." It is instead lively and resourceful, because it "plunges" and "pierces" through the sky and the soil i.e. the world that had enchained him in powerlessness. Cesaire's poem therefore illustrates the historic development of the identity and the culture of the black man in the West as a means of affirming the pride and the heritage of his cultural values.

The basic concept of Negritude therefore characterised the collective identity of suffering of Africans in the Diaspora who shared the same historic experience of subjugation. According to Césaire's poem, Negritude stood to recognise and accept a common history, culture and destiny. It therefore exposed the common position of black people as far as the slave trade, Colonialism and Western racism were concerned, thereby aiming at unifying black consciousness. Césaire's version of Negritude presented a model that symbolised the continued struggle for the freedom of black people both politically and historically, even if it focused more on the cultural aspect of the struggle.

Aimé Césaire's ideas were later adopted by Léopold Sédar Senghor, but he was said to have modified the interpretations attributed to Césaire's *The Return to the Native Land.* In his writings and debates, he accentuated the permanent and eternal existence of the values of black culture. In *The Poetry of Action: Conversation with Mohamed Aziza, Paris*[52], Senghor gave perhaps the most comprehensive version of what Negritude meant for him:

la clameur du jour
ma negritude n'est pas une taie d'eau morte sur l'œil
mort de la terre
ma negritude n'est ni une tour ni une cathedrale
elle plonge dans la chair rouge du sol
elle plonge dans la chair ardente du ciel
elle troue l'accablement opaque de sa droite patience.

[52] *"La Poésie de l'Action : Conversation avec Mohamed Aziza"*, Paris, 1980.

Negritude has two aspects: objective and subjective. The objective aspect is the total values of black civilisation, of which is the sense of communion, the gift of analogical image, the gift of rhythm ... it is a symbiosis between intelligence and the soul, spirit and matter .... In its subjective aspect, Negritude is also a kind of will and manner to live the values that exist.[53]

He visibly outlined two aspects of Negritude: "objective and subjective," attributing the objective aspect, which according to him represented "the total value of the civilisation of the black man," to himself, and the subjective aspect that concerns the will to live with these values to Aimé Césaire, which according to him, was natural because the ancestors of Césaire had been deported to the New World. His five-volume work, *Liberty*[54] further detailed his notion of Negritude in the form of symbolism. Senghor constructed a typology of what he called the "eternal. black soul" structured on "emotion, rhythm and humour." He continuously defended and developed the idea of an "African personality", especially in his work: *Négritude et Humanisme*.[55] The bulk of Senghor's Negritude attempted to reverse the stigmatisation of black people commonplace in 19th century racialism. For him, race is a reality without signifying the relative "purity" of any one race, contrary to what was promoted in some Western literature.[56] Senghorian Negritude principally contained cultural and civilisational values, but he rejected all forms of opposition between black and white peoples as well as the notion of the exclusivity of race. He accepted that there was a difference between the races, but again that this difference did not denote "inferiority" or "antagonism." He believed in the expression of traditions, incarnated in the thoughts and institutions of African

---

[53]*La négritude se présente sous deux aspects : objectif et subjectif. Sous son aspect objectif, c'est l'ensemble des valeurs de la civilisation du monde noir, dont le sens de la communion, le don de l'image analogique, le don du rythme [...], c'est une symbiose entre l'intelligence et l'âme, l'esprit et la matière [...]. Dans son aspect subjectif, la négritude est aussi une certaine volonté et une certaine manière de vivre les valeurs que voilà.* (Senghor, "La Poésie de l'Action")

[54]*Liberté*

[55]*Negritude and Humanism*

[56]Joseph Arthur de Gobineau's "Racial Theories (Essay on the Inequality of Human Races"(1853-1855), Lucien Levy-Bruhl's concept of a prelogical "primitive mentality," and fictional works such as Paul Morand's stereotype-laden novel, "*Magie noire*" (1928).

societies, but did not wish for a return to outmoded customs. Senghor considered Negritude as a cultural foundation on which a modern African society could be built with its own traditional, artistic and literary trends. The manner in which he interpreted Negritude became a model for many writers, but he was equally accused of formulating his own reading to serve him as a political purpose at a time he was President of Senegal. The object of his interpretation, accordingly, was to "rectify" the purposeful perceptive eye of the world especially that of the West on black people. Through Negritude, Senghor wished to affirm himself as a black man; and to obtain that assertion he postulated that Negritude represented the civilisation and culture of black people, while rejecting the idea of opposition, thereby invoking the idea of assimilation, but without altering one's own personality.

It is essential to note that whatever definition is attributed to Negritude, it could in no way escape the notion of refusal and/or resistance especially in this era of post-Colonialism. It is also interesting to compare the notion of assimilation present in Senghor's version of Negritude, presumably, to the white man's culture, without expressing the other way round, which logically suggested the superiority of the one to the other. Indeed the institutions of slavery and Colonialism were based on this very idea. In the end the two aspects of Negritude that Senghor tried to disengage: the objective (Senghor) and the subjective (Césaire), were inseparable, even if there seemed to be some distinction between them. Senghor's version gave precedence to the cultural aspect; it also instinctively engaged a parallel battle, and suggests that the black man amongst whites had to fight and manifest his personality and culture without being antagonistic because there was no way of concealing his identity that could enable him to escape racism. Jean Paul Sartre pointed this out in Senghor's anthology, *Black Orpheus* that he had prefaced in 1948:

> …a Jew, a white among whites, can deny that he is a Jew, declaring himself a man among men. The black cannot deny that he is black nor claim for himself an abstract, colourless humanity: he is black. Thus he is driven to authenticity: insulted, enslaved, he raises himself up. He picks up the word "black" ["Nègre"] that they had thrown at him like a stone; he asserts his blackness, facing the white man, with pride. (4)[57]

---

[57] … *un Juif, blanc parmi les Blancs, peut nier qu'il soit juif, se déclarer un homme parmi les*

Sartre's point of view establishes the concept of Negritude pertaining to black identity. He remarked on the concept of a racial essence in Negritudian literature, but that a "Negre" in the midst of white people can in no way hide his identity and condition. He was therefore obliged to accept his colour and his nature. He then used the term "Negre," a term that had been offensively used towards him, to show his pride, which he qualified as "antiracist racism" (Ibid).

Just as Pan-Africanism, Negritude provoked different critiques in the form of ideological debates especially from black historians and academicians in both the Anglophone and the Francophone worlds, particularly pertaining to its essence to African Nationalism and reconstruction.

In his work *Black Skin, White Masks*, Frantz Fanon criticised Senghor's expression: "Emotion is black as Reason is Hellenic," accusing him of glorifying the unreasonable, which made the process regressive (177). Both Fanon and Chinua Achebe rejected Sartre's denial of race as an integral component of Negritude and black identity. Sartre had viewed Negritude as a phenomenon that would eventually disappear once the black and white racial conflict was resolved (www.enotes.com).

Most Anglophone African writers considered Negritude largely as a politicised and ideological movement.

Kwame Nkrumah critiqued Negritude as an ideology that:

…consists in a mere literary affection and style which piles word upon word and image upon image with occasional reference to Africa and things that are related to Africa. …a vague brotherhood based on a criterion of colour, or on the idea that Africans have no reasoning but only sensitivity. (nkrumah.net)

Nkrumah here makes reference to Senghor's celebrated term: "Emotion is Black as Reason is Hellenic."[58] In the same manner he opposed Negritude to the "African genius," which according to him

---

hommes. Le nègre ne peut pas nier qu'il soit nègre ni réclamer pour lui cette abstraite humanité incolore : il est noir. Ainsi est-il acculé à l'authenticité : insulté, asservi, il se redresse, il réclame le mot « nègre » qu'on lui a jeté comme une pierre, il se revendique comme noir, en face du blanc, dans la fierté.
[58] *L'émotion est nègre, comme la raison Hellène.*

was: "something positive, our socialist conception of society, the efficiency and validity of our traditional statecraft, our highly developed code of morals, our hospitality and our purposeful energy." (Ibid) Kwame ingenuously rejected any positive role of Negritude in African liberation and reconstruction. For him it is apologetic and undynamic, and therefore not very productive to African reconstruction.

Wole Soyinka criticised a perceived cultural Imperialism of the Francophone African intellectuals, and argued that, "the tiger does not stalk about crying his tigritude." For Soyinka:

...Negritude was essential to the people that formulated the philosophy of renewed conscience of their black identity, but like the majority of movements that start on the sidewalk of cafés, it is largely artificial and rhetoric. It is also exaggerated because the people who needed this reclamation were immigrants; they had no relation with the major part of their countries. In other words the African people have never lost their Negritude, never. (...) the situation in Africa is very different from what it was in the United States. Here Negritude or the black personality and conscience, was not only a historic phenomenon, it had to be a brusque revolutionary activity. (qtd. in Jeyifo 10)[59]

Soyinka noticeably expresses the passiveness embedded in especially Senghorian Négritude and the view that Negritude belongs to colonial ideology, by the fact that it is not reformatory in a historical perspective. He argues that Negritude was formulated to awaken the awareness and identity of black people of the period, for this reason it has less importance for the African of today. Even if it was obviously attached to the imperfections of the past that were inherent to humanity, Africa's innocence in the colonial period should be affirmed. If Soyinka accepts that Negritude is a product of the Diaspora in its rhetoric, and that it has favoured the emergence of

---

[59] ... *la Négritude était essentielle au peuple qui avait formulé cette philosophie de la conscience renouvelée de leur identité noire, mais comme la plupart des mouvements qui commencent sur le trottoir des cafés, c'est largement artificiel et rhétorique. C'est aussi exagéré parce que les gens qui avaient besoin de cette revendication étaient des immigrés; ils n'avaient pas de relation avec la majeure partie de leur pays. En d'autres mots le peuple africain n'a jamais perdu sa négritude, jamais. Maintenant la situation en Afrique est très différente de ce qu'elle était aux Etats-Unis. Ici la négritude ou la personnalité, la conscience noire, n'était pas seulement un phénomène historique. Il devait être une activité révolutionnaire brusque.*

African leaders on the continent, it however according to him affirms African reality differently.

In the Francophone world the general critique of Negritude broadly followed Leopold Sédar Senghor's concept and centred on the supposedly "African" features of intuition, emotion and artistic inventiveness as opposed to a Western and/or "Hellenic" reasoning. The Guadeloupean writer Maryse Conde criticised the idea of a return to Africa. In her article in the *"Revue de littérature comparée, "*entitled *Negritude Cesairienne, Negritude Senghorienne* , she drew attention to Cesaire's version of Negritude, and offered a sharp warning against fetishising blackness:

> The black ("Negre") does not exist . . . [Negritude] is a sentimental and empty trap. Starting from an illusory "racial" community founded upon a heritage of suffering, it obliterates the true problems that have always been of a political, social, and economic nature . . . Our liberation will come through the knowledge that there will never be any Blacks ("Negres"). There has only ever been human exploitation. (413)

The implication of this criticism is that Negritude should not remain a simple call of black identity and the valorisation of its artistic traits, the sufferings must also serve to enlighten the very constructiveness for "blackness" itself.

Jean Bernabe, Patrick Chamoiseau, and Raphael Confiant all criticised Cesaire's Negritude for making Africa "mythical," pointing out the heterogeneous cultural status of the Caribbean: French, Chinese, Hindu, Amerindian, and African elements.

The pioneers of Negritude also tended to present themselves as Surrealists which more or less compromised its originality and made it more a means than a goal by the fact that Surrealism was more an artistic phenomenon. However the source of Negritude, in spite of these flaws, rests on the African who expresses it in its concept, myth and images, by the notion that Black people all over are discriminated against and humiliated, but demands in an inextinguishable cry, their dignity as men.[60] (Bâ vii).

---

[60]Les idées de tous les Nègres discriminés, affamés, humiliés, mais revendiquant, dans un cri inextinguible, leur dignité d'homme.

Senghor's version of Negritude affirming black culture and civilisation, and refuting confrontation with Western culture is merely simplistic. However due to its defence of black culture and civilisation, if one cannot qualify it as nationalist in a purely African context and need for liberation and reconstruction, one cannot either deprive it of a nationalist significance. There is more than a simple nuance between Negritude and Pan-Africanism in West Africa as forms of African Nationalism such as they have been defined and analysed. The basic difference is that the former was based more on a cultural phenomenon and the latter, purely political. Negritude is nationalistic but not nationalistic enough in the context of effective African reconstruction.

Interpreters of West African Nationalism.

A study of Pan-Africanism and Negritude as nationalistic instruments of reconstruction and development in West Africa requires looking into the personalities and views of Kwame Nkrumah and Léopold Sédar Senghor.

Both were intellectuals, statesmen and nationalists on the African front. They were both the first Presidents of their respective countries after Independence, and had each led anti-colonial and anti-racist battles, but each had employed a radically different method.

Therefore, there might be enormous differences between the two protagonists concerning their roles in African liberation and reconstruction, but there were similarities as well. They were even more like twins, but twins with different conducts, because they were brought up by different guardians. In Anglophone and Francophone West Africa, President Nkrumah of Ghana and President Senghor of Senegal were thus indisputably pioneers of Pan-Africanism and Negritude respectively.

Apart from their ideologies, it is necessary to study their behaviour with power and government in their respective countries, to situate their roles in post-colonial reconstruction and development.

In this section we have essentially explored the contribution of the two protagonists in West African Nationalism and their roles in reconstruction.

Kwame Nkrumah

We have learnt that Nkrumah's philosophy of Nationalism was attached to creating an African Central Government as a step towards total liberation and reconstruction. A close study of his works shows that he was amongst the main protagonists of West African Nationalism in a global context. His education in the United States and England gave him the chance to study American history and politics in detail. From this he became aware of the strength and advantages of the North American model of federalism, thereby envisaging that Ghana and indeed the whole of Africa could benefit from the North American system of politics and government.

Nkrumah started as an author in the United States, publishing *Education and Nationalism in Africa,* and *Towards Colonial Freedom* in 1943, pamphlets he released after his contribution to the Foundation of African Students in the United States and Canada, of which he became president. His involvement in this association marked his first engagement in politics. He seriously denounced colonisation as a means for the West to deprive Africans of their natural rights. His most important role was membership of the West African National Secretariat, (WANS)[61] thereby becoming very quickly a key player in the transformation and transfer of Pan-Negroism from the Americas to Pan-Africanism in Anglophone West Africa. His relationship with the Jamaican, Marcus Garvey had a great deal of influence on his vision of the world; visibly Nkrumah's Nationalism was purely revolutionary. Amongst African nationalists, most observers considered his image and position with regards to African integration and reconstruction as the most solid and the most operational. Nkrumah's Pan-Africanism was authentically anti-imperial and for him, only unity could save the African continent from imperialist encroachment. His works and declarations showed the vigour of his idea of unity in post-colonial Africa:

> If we are to remain free, if we are to enjoy the full benefits of Africa's rich resources, we must unite to plan for our total defence and the full exploitation of our material and human means in the full interest of all our people. 'To go it alone' will limit our horizons, curtail our expectations and threaten our liberty. (*Africa Must Unite* XVII)

> If we do not formulate plans for unity and take active steps to form political union, we will soon be fighting and warring amongst ourselves with imperialists and colonialists standing behind the screen and pulling vicious wires, to cut each other's throats for the sake of their diabolical purposes in Africa. (Speech at the closing session of the Casablanca Conference, 7 January 1961.)[62]

> There is no time to waste. The longer we wait the stronger will be the hold on Africa of neo-Colonialism and Imperialism. A Union Government for Africa does not mean the loss of sovereignty by

---

[61] The West African National Secretariat was a Pan-Africanist movement that Kwame Nkrumah, I.T.A Wallace-Johnson (elected Chairman), Bankole Akpata, Kojo Botsio and Bankole Awooner (elected President) established in December 1945, immediately after the Manchester Pan-African Congress. Kwame became the new organisation's Secretary-General. The majority of WANS' members were also members of the West African Students' Union.

[62] Quoted in *Axioms of Kwame Nkrumah*, 9.

independent African States. A Union Government will rather strengthen the sovereignty of individual States within the union. (Speech made in Accra, May 1964.)[63]

We cannot save ourselves except through the unity of our continent based on common action through a Continental Union Government. Only a united Africa under a Union Government can cure us of our economic ills and lift us out our despair and frustration. (Speech at the Cairo Summit Conference, 26 July 1964)[64]

I am convinced that the forces making for unity far outweigh those which divide us. In meeting fellow Africans from all the parts of the continent I am constantly impressed by how much we have in common, it is something which goes far deeper. I can best describe it as a sense of one-ness in that we are Africans. ((*Africa Must Unite* 132)

If Africa was united, no major power block would attempt to subdue it by limited war because, from the very nature of limited war what can be achieved by it is itself limited. It is only where small states exist that it is possible, by landing a few thousand marines or by financing a mercenary force to secure a decisive result. ... A continent like Africa, however much it increases its agricultural output, will not benefit unless it is sufficiently and economically united to force the developed world to pay it a fair price for its cash crops (*Neo-Colonialism* XI).

Visibly the most important point in Nkrumah's philosophy as far as sustainable reconstruction in post-colonial Africa was concerned, was the fight against Imperialism as witnessed by his numerous declarations. But, for him, this battle could only be won if the post-colonial African States abandoned the geopolitical structures set up by the West at the Berlin Conference and formed a unity government with a central command: *Africa Must Unite*, as he coined in one of his major works, to exploit its natural resources and assure its own socio-economic development. The economic problems could only be surmounted through unity of all the African peoples. Nkrumah counselled Africans against the dangers of failure to institute a unity government. The continent would lose its independence, because lack

---

[63] Quoted in *Axioms of Kwame Nkrumah*, 13.
[64] Quoted in *Axioms of Kwame Nkrumah*, 14.

of political unity would generate inter-State and civil wars which in turn would encourage and facilitate the interference of the imperialists in African affairs. Unity therefore should strengthen the sovereignty of member States instead of weakening it. This showed that Nkrumah was mindful of the concerns, the scepticism and fear that surrounded the immediate post-colonial African leaders about losing their sovereignty in the event of the States coming together into a federal State.

However, some observers believed that he stressed African unity to a point that many of his compatriots suspected that he was trying to become the supreme leader of Africa, and therefore the most powerful man on the continent:

> ... the problem with Kwame Nkrumah's proposal, was a question of leadership, because everybody thought that Kwame Nkrumah was only proposing this so he would be President of Africa. You see, that's what those people were thinking, they did not see what he was trying to say. He was trying to promote African Unity; if we had to compete with Europeans we had to be one. That was reasonable, but what people were hearing was that he wanted to become the head of Africa. (Interview, 20 June 2007)

When Nkrumah took power in the Gold Coast in 1957, the majority of African countries were under colonial rule. He was one of the first Prime Ministers of independent Sub-Saharan African countries. This position might have given him the impression of being one of the natural leaders of the future Federation of African States. He thence was seen as a model for the other nationalist leaders. This likely piloted him to the point of nearly neglecting the domestic affairs of his country, which probably provoked his downfall.

Nkrumah's position can be summarised in two aspects: Africans must unite to save their continent, or continue to disunite, disintegrate, and put themselves in a state of weakness and capitulation before Imperialism. For him, the more Africans wasted time the more the enemy got stronger, which would retard the aspirations of the peoples of Africa or even almost terminally paralyse it. He was opposed to the idea of regional integration as a step towards continental unity. He believed that regional economic and political organisations led Africans to nowhere because they yielded too little for Africa's reconstruction efforts. Only unity of all the

African peoples under the leadership of a central or federal government that would carry out the politics of scientific Socialism could produce real sustainable socio-economic growth as a factor of reconstruction and development on the continent.

After the inception of the OAU, of which he was one of the main architects, he criticised its charter. For him the difference of opinion at the 1963 conference in Addis Ababa affected the project of African integration all through the existence of the OAU:

> The lack of provision for an All-African High Command to give teeth to the organisation, meant that the OAU suffered from the start from inherent weaknesses. There was much talk of the inviolability of [national] sovereignty,... Most of our national frontiers are relics of Colonialism, and irrelevant within the context of the African nation. (*Africa Must Unite* 43)

Here Kwame's use of the term "nation" sends us back to our definition of Nationalism in the African context that all the African peoples share the same experience of exploitation as one family with the same lineage.

As far as the administration of his country was concerned, Nkrumah governed Ghana in a manner considered by many as autocratic (ghanaian-chronicle.com).

He was accused of being so spiritually preoccupied by African unity that he almost ignored the principles of democracy in his country. After Independence in Ghana, Nkrumah was accused of investing too much of Ghana's resources in the project of African unity. (ibid) Between 1957 and 1960, he organised two Pan-African congresses and travelled all over Africa to promote his ideas. When France reluctantly and grudgingly gave Independence to Guinea (Conakry) in 1958, Nkrumah accorded a credit of 25 million dollars to the Guinean leader, Ahmed Sékou Touré. He was said to have outlawed opposition, and some people accused him of being more concerned with the prestige of power and leadership, and that he believed that African unity would personally be more beneficial to him than promoting socio-economic development and the principles of democracy in his country, on the basis of which he had fought for Independence, especially when he was "crowned" "*Osagyefo*."[65] When

---

[65]According to June Milne who worked with Nkrumah up to his death, Nkrumah did

he was elected to the position of Prime Minister in 1952 by the Legislative Assembly, many people later accused him of being autocratic in his administration.

1960 was an important year for democracy in Ghana; Nkrumah organised a referendum in July that some observers considered as having been fraudulent. Ghana voted for the country to become a Republic and Nkrumah successively became President in 1964. He was subsequently accused of banning all opposition and controlling legislative and judicial powers. In April 1961 Nkrumah was said to have forced his rivals to resign, then arrested many of them, and then expelled British army officers who were training the Ghanaian army. In August 1962, while he was returning from a visit to Upper Volta (now Burkina Faso), Nkrumah made an unscheduled stop at the village of Kulungugu in northern Ghana. He was attacked with a grenade as he stopped to speak to a group of children. He was wounded and four people died in that attack. Consequently he took draconian measures, naturally, to protect himself. He was said to have accused his former boss, Joseph Danquah of the United Gold Coast Convention (UGCC) of complicity with terrorists and sent him to jail, where Danquah died the following year. Nkrumah ended up being overthrown in a coup d'état led by Major-General Joseph Ankrah in 1966, while away in Beijing on a mediation tour of the Vietnam War. The founder of the modern Ghanaian State was then denounced as a dictator who "was only interested in power and prestige." For Akwasi A. Afrifa, "Nkrumah could have been a great man. He started well… Somewhere down the line, however… he developed a strange love for absolute power." (Kent 41).

Some observers, however, expressed the view that Nkrumah's ultimate desire was a free united Africa. Sékou Touré, in a speech to the Guinean nation after Nkrumah's death in exile, expressed the view that:

---

not crown himself neither did he seek the title Osagyefo "… the word has frequently been translated by non-Ghanaians to mean Redeemer, as proof that Nkrumah encouraged a personality cult." But the real meaning of the term is "Victorious Leader"…bestowed on Nkrumah by the Asantehene, King of the Ashanti people. It had been used for one of the greatest warrior chiefs. The Asantehene considered that Nkrumah well deserved the title, having achieved so much for Ghana and for Africa. It was considered fitting that Nkrumah should be addressed as Osagyefo rather than as President, a non-African title.

Kwame Nkrumah was one of the men who marked the destiny of mankind fighting for freedom and dignity. Kwame Nkrumah lives and will forever because Africa, which is grateful to him, will live forever. The combatants of all races and colours, fighting for Independence and solidarity of all the nations of the world, will continue to live and fight for Kwame Nkrumah's ideals. (qtd. in Milne 264)

The African Union launched the African Renaissance Campaign on Africa Day, May 25, 2010 to commemorate the centenary of Kwame Nkrumah's birth. The campaign largely aimed at broadening the discourse on African Renaissance across disciplines, and strengthening the African Union's quest for a renascence of the African continent especially the socio-economic and cultural domains. On 21st September 2009, Ghanaians and Africans all over the world celebrated the centenary of Nkrumah's birth. The Ghanaian president, John Atta Mills urged the nation to demonstrate "collective pride" in what he named "Founder's Day." He portrayed Nkrumah as the man who "lit the flame that blazed a liberation struggle of the African continent." This collective pride has surely been strengthened by Ghanaians all over the world and Africans indeed, after Ghana's U20 World Cup Championship win over Brazil on October 16, 2009 and Ghana's subsequent, however unsuccessful semi-final bid in the 2010 World Cup tournament in South Africa.

Léopold Sédar Senghor

Léopold Sédar Senghor originally exposed his nationalist aspirations in Paris. But, as Sylvia Washington Bà noted in her work *The Concept of Négritude in the Poetry of Léopold Sédar Senghor:*

...the germs of Senghor's Negritude, which constituted the basis of his Nationalism, could be traced as far back as in 1922 when he was a student in Collège Liberman in Dakar, (colonial Senegal). In spite of the fact that he identified himself with colonial French "Liberty, Equality and Fraternity," Senghor disagreed with his professor, Father Lalouze, who denied the existence of a valid African civilization, even to the point of calling them savages. (8)

It was later during his studies at Louis le-Grand High School in Paris at the beginning of the 1930s that Senghor met personalities like

Aimé Césaire, Alain Locke, and Claude Mackay which led him to nourish more affection for his African heritage. Aimé Césaire later introduced him to literature, (Black American poetry and the works of the Harlem Renaissance of the 1920s, such as the works of James Weldon Johnson, Frank Marshal David, Countee Cullen, and Langson Hughes.) He also discovered other publications such as *The Crisis, National Urban League, Opportunité,*[66] and *New Negro* which was edited by Alain Locke. He was also attracted by the writings of the German ethnologist Léo Frobenius, who revealed "a lyrical version of Africanity" to the world. Senghor thereafter remained attached to the West Indian intellectuals of the *Revue du monde noir.*[67] These contacts with black students and writers encouraged him to strongly portray himself as black or simply as an African. With the aid of Léon Damas and Aimé Césaire, Senghor published *L'étudiant Noir,*[68] for the first time in 1934, for all the black students in Paris, a journal considered as the vector of his Negritude. In that journal, he formulated his vision of politics as a manifestation and an aspect of culture. In 1939 he published an article entitled *Ce que l'homme noir apporte,*[69] after having passed at his second attempt the examination to qualify as a teacher and his subsequent nomination as a teacher of French language, grammar and literature at Tours in 1939. In 1964, *Le Seuil* published a collection of Senghor's writings on Negritude, humanism, and socialism entitled *Liberté.*[70] This was considered the most obvious of his version of Negritude, notably the well-known aphorism: "Emotion is Black as Reason is Hellenic."[71] In spite of becoming a professional politician and President of his native Senegal, he underlined that poetry was his major contribution to African culture, unlike Nkrumah whose version of Nationalism was predominantly politico-economic. Senghor identified "culture and civilisation" and considered poetry as a means through which one could disseminate a message to the world, and contribute to universal civilisation.

We have seen that Senghor's version of Nationalism that he expressed through Negritude was first of all cultural and literary. He

---

[66] Opportunity.

[67] Review of the black world

[68] The Black Student.

[69] What the black man contributes.

[70] Liberty

[71] *L'émotion est nègre, comme la raison Hellène.*

was also a central character of the Francophonie; and despite underlining the notion of racism that was prevalent in his time, he differentiated himself from other African nationalists of his time in his attitude towards racism. Of course he denounced racism and European colonisation in Africa all through his writings, but he equally campaigned for reconciliation and forgiveness, which had almost no place in Nkrumah's Nationalism. The theory of Senghor's Nationalism was based on three principal ideologies: African Socialism, Negritude and the Francophonie. We have seen that his ideology of Negritude consisted of the cultural values of black people, values that according to him should promote African integration. Like Nkrumah, Senghor denounced Colonialism and the slave trade. However he asked God to forgive France for what she had inflicted on Africa:

> Kill it, Lord, for I must continue on my journey
> And I want to pray especially for France.
> Lord, among white nations, place France at the Father's right hand.
> Oh, I know she, too, is Europe, that she has snatched my children
> Like a cattle-rustling brigand from the north
> To fatten her lands with sugarcane and cotton...
> Yes, Lord, forgive France...
> That has turned my Mesopotamia and my Congo
> Into a vast cemetery under the white sun.[72] (*Hosties noires* 94-95)

Some observers might have attributed his prayers for peace and reconciliatory stance to the weight of his spiritual devotion; others might have interpreted them as simply insincere and inconsiderate. It is true that if the Lord had to forgive the actors for their collective sin in the slave trade and Colonialism, it would be desirable for the sake

---

[72]*Tue-le Seigneur, car il me faut poursuivre mon chemin,*
Et je veux prier singulièrement pour la France.
Seigneur, parmi les nations blanches, place la France à la droite du Père.
Oh! je sais bien qu'elle aussi est l'Europe, qu'elle m'a ravi les enfants
Comme un brigand du Nord des bœufs,
Pour engraisser ses terres à cannes et coton, ...
Oui Seigneur, pardonne à la France...
Et de ma Mésopotamie, de mon Congo, ils ont fait un grand cimetière sous le soleil blanc.

of spiritual justice or reconciliation and humanity to collectively put all Europe and North America and indeed any parties involved, on the right hand side instead of singly forgiving France. What was more, Léopold Sédar Senghor had not asked Africans if they wanted to pray to the Lord to forgive France exclusively for the wrong she had done to Africa, and punish Britain, Spain, Portugal or any other party involved. In the end Senghor's prayer for peace on behalf of Africans has difficulty escaping moral hypocrisy. Nkrumah had never prayed to the Lord to forgive the perpetrators of the slave trade and Colonialism in Africa; Marcus Garvey would have cursed or disowned him. He instead pleaded to Africans to unite and stand strong against the imperialists, and surely to avenge the wrongs done to them.

If Senghor's behaviour distinguished him from his Anglophone counterpart, it was probably because his upbringing was different from most African nationalists of his time. As a student at *Collège Liberman*[73] in Dakar, Senghor was the only black student amongst French students. In Louis-le-Grand High School in Paris he was again the only black student amidst white students. After leaving his native Senegal in 1928 at 22, a relatively early age and spending most of his time with Claude and Georges Pompidou, a former Presidential couple of France, he returned to Senegal over the age of 40. The colonial system in which Senghor's Senegal found itself was also radically different from the others. Senegal occupied a special place in the French colonial administration in West Africa. From 1848, France accorded citizenship[74] to the inhabitants of Dakar, Gorée, Rufisque and Saint Louis. In 1916 full French citizenship was extended to the inhabitants of the port of Dakar and to the other three Communes: Saint-Louis, Gorée and Rufisque, which gave them the right to elect municipal councillors. Blaise Diagne, the main advocate behind the change, became the first African deputy in the French National Assembly. From this date to independence, the

---

[73] Liberman Primary School.
[74] The four oldest colonial towns in French West Africa were the Four Communes (*quatre vieilles*) of Senegal. In 1848, the Second Republic in France accorded the rights of full French citizenship to the inhabitants of Dakar, Gorée, Rufisque and Saint Louis. Natives of these towns were technically native French citizens, but some legal and social barriers prevented the full exercise of their rights, especially those considered by authorities as "full blooded" Africans. It was only in 1916 that *originaires* or natives were granted full voting rights while maintaining legal protections.

deputies of the Four Communes were always Africans, and were at the forefront of the struggle. His successors were Galandou Diouf, Lamine Guèye and Léopold Sédar Senghor himself. At the peak of colonisation then, Senegal elected deputies in the French National Assembly, just like the DOMTOM[75] today. That was unimaginable in the British colonial system.

Dr. Salawu Adewuni has rightfully pointed out in his electronic article entitled *West African Nationalism Rediscovered*, that: "...The French system of administering her colonies was the assimilation method first applied in St. Louis and Gorée and later in Dakar and Rufisque. The policy was extended to all French West African colonies..." (10). However his idea that the principle behind this whole notion of assimilation was inspired by the ideals of "Liberty, Fraternity and Equality" of the French Revolution is defective. This Liberty Equality and Fraternity ideal of the French Revolution was important to the French but practically unapplied in African colonies. In fact the very principle of colonisation in general, especially considering the French policy of forced labour in its colonies, terribly contradicted the notion of French Liberty, Equality and Fraternity. This is exactly analogous with the gist of Thomas Jefferson's Declaration of Independence for the thirteen English colonies in North America in 1776 that told King George III of England that the American people: "...hold these truths to be self-evident, that all men are created equal, that they are endowed by their Creator with certain unalienable Rights that among these are Life, Liberty and the pursuit of Happiness."

The irony was that at the time of this declaration? Thomas Jefferson, George Washington and almost all the Founding Fathers defending American Independence and demonstrating the endowment of unalienable rights for all by nature, were keeping and working black slaves in their backyards. This showed that this moral reasoning based on the notion of freedom and equality whether the French version of Liberty, Equality, Fraternity, or the American declaration of "unalienable Rights of Life, Liberty and the pursuit of

---

[75] The collectivity of lands that are under French sovereignty situated outside the metropole. The accronym signifies Overseas Department — Overseas territory - *Département d'outre mer- Terretoire d'outre-mer*. The DOM-TOM includes: Guadeloupe, Martinique, French Guiana, Réunion.

Happiness," was flawed, phoney and insincere unless they were for white people only, which they did not stipulate.

However the real notion of French "Assimilation"[76] developed by France in most of the 20th century, was based on the idea that the colonised would eventually be integrated into the French system and adopt the "superior" culture of France to become French. Senghor was part of this group of Senegalese representatives and therefore part of this assimilation trial. British colonies in West Africa had never had a voice in Parliament, neither in the House of Commons nor in the House of Lords, not even in the administration of the colonies of which they were part, before the 20th century.

Senghor's idea of African Socialism was based on a universal approach, which went round a nationalist perspective. For Nkrumah the struggle between Africa and its colonisers was a struggle between political and socio-economic exploiters and the exploited, therefore African unity must be essentially anti-imperialist. Senghor, just like Nkrumah, Patrice Lumumba and Julius Nyerere was against the Balkanisation of Africa, especially French West Africa, which would create States too small and too weak to be viable. The federation of Mali, between Senegal and French Sudan (now Mali) just before their joint Independence, symbolised this fear. A disposition in the Constitution of the Republic of Senegal introduced by Senghor, stipulating that Senegal was ready to renounce its sovereignty to realise African unity confirms this point. However, for Senghor, colonisation belonged to the past because Africa was now independent, and in that outlook, orientating African unity solely to an anti-colonial struggle made it unrealistic and fragile. Senghor was a defender of cultural hybridity and a partisan of African unity, but unity accompanied by strong and cordial relations with the West.

His idea thus presented Africa as complementary to Europe, and his vision bluntly ignored the distinction between Colonialism and Imperialism. His theory of Nationalism based on the notion of complementarity seemed to be simply stimulating and tempting, and

---

[76] In spite of the right to citizenship most of the African population of these towns were referred to as *originaires*, Africans born into the commune, but who continued using African and or Islamic law. A few Africans from the four communes who managed to pursue higher education and were ready to give up their legal protections were termed the Evolved (*Évolués*) and were nominally granted full French citizenship, including the right to vote. Despite this legal framework, the *Évolués* still faced substantial discrimination in Africa and the metropolitan France alike.

it ignored the reality of African reconstruction in the perspective of sustainable socio-economic development. It is true that Africa cannot base its reconstruction efforts on perpetual antagonism with its former colonisers or with the West at large in this era of post-Colonialism and globalisation, but it cannot either ignore anti-imperial rhetoric and/or actions even if it was not the only continent to be colonised. Colonialism is formally over, but Imperialism is still present in Africa. Moreover most strong modern nations, such as the United States of America, partly derived their politico-economic strength and power out of anti-imperial struggle. Imperialism is still an encroaching danger for Africa just as it was in the 1900s.

When he was President of Senegal between 1960 and 1980, Senghor in his turn did not escape the syndrome that affected most immediate post-colonial African leaders, in particular the key players in the fight against Colonialism. He presented an image of a humanist, democratic and intellectual politician, but he sometimes exercised his political power with unnecessary authority even if it did not attain the dimension of pure dictatorship. At a moment of his presidency, between 1960 and 1974 President Senghor had accordingly governed Senegal:

...under one-party rule, the authority and stability of Senegal's "presidential Monarchy" were based on personal patronage that pervaded the legislature, judiciary, bureaucracy, and ruling Parti Socialiste (PS), while integrating a desperate group of communal leaders .(...) the leadership of the PS state chose to avoid political violence and military repression...undertake political liberalisation to legitimize their besieged regime, while assuming their continued tenure in power by controlling the scope and implementation of democratic reforms their patrimonial relationships. (Beck 2)

Senghor was also accused of being more attached to the colonial institution, as Diouf Mamadou argues here:

The institutional environment that the new state puts in place confirms the continuity of the colonial system; the ancient forms (colonial) of power and the leadership have consolidated themselves by investing directly or by intermediate clients in the new authority and influence. The coalition of the evolved and the natives established itself in a strategic socio-Professional group in the

79

construction of a very strong centralised state of colonial rationality. (248)[77]

This argument could be confirmed by the fact that Senghor had employed a large number of French technical advisers[78] to the detriment of the Senegalese national budget. During Senghor's Presidency, the opposition were said to have been sometimes suppressed and thrown into clandestinity "or victim of police bullying... of arbitrary arrests... In a nutshell power... was arbitrary that did not allow the opposition to express themselves freely and publicly."[79] (Tune 7)

President Senghor was accused of not tolerating the opposition, which made Senegal a one-party State. He was said to have forced his Prime Minister, Mamadou Dia, to resign in 1962 and to subsequently imprison him until 1974 amidst allegations that he was planning to stage a military coup to overthrow him. At this juncture one might well ask about Senghor's Catholic spirit of reconciliation, humanism and prayers. It was only in 1970, when he probably realised the need for political change because of the dissatisfaction of the population that he reinstituted the post of Prime Minister and appointed Abdou Diouf, and subsequently authorised lawyer Abdoulaye Wade to form the first legal political party of opposition. Senghor had therefore not introduced multi-party politics voluntarily, but because of the pressure on him created by dissatisfaction in the country. In May 1968 students went on strike; they were followed by workers and the government could not contain the explosion of anger. Even with the institution of multi-party politics, his government did not initially want to accept the word "opposition." Consequently Wade chose to call his Senegalese Democratic Party (PDS)[80], the party of contribution.

---

[77]*L'environnement institutionnel que le nouvel État mit en place autorise à affirmer que la continuité coloniale fut maintenue; ... La coalition des évolués et des originaires s'érigea en groupe socio-professionnel stratégique dans la construction d'un État très fortement centralisé et doté d'une rationalité coloniale.*

[78]*Conseillers techniques français.*

[79]*...ou victime des brimades policières, ... d'arrestations arbitraires... Bref le pouvoir...fut un pouvoir arbitraire qui ne permettait pas à l'opposition de s'exprimer librement et publiquement. »*

[80]*Parti démocratique sénégalais.*

However despite these authoritative tendencies, Senghor did not impose himself as an absolute dictator and this distinguished him from many leaders. Many believed that Senghor's humanist values and perhaps the image he wanted to portray to the world, did not allow him to institute unlimited authority in the sense of absolute dictatorship. Senghor had never constantly employed violence in his power, and in spite of the fact that Senegal experienced very little economic growth during the 20 years of his rule, the country enjoyed relative political stability in Africa. Jacques Louis Hymans, Professor of History at the San Francisco State University, described Senghor as a "living symbol of the possible synthesis of what appears irreconcilable: he is African as he is European, as much a poet as a politician… as much a revolutionary as a traditionalist." (Kent 57). In reality Senghor's politics and governance yielded mixed results. Political stability in Senegal during his rule was accredited to his relative humanism and especially to his political and intellectual talents as Sheldon Gellar summarised here:

> Senghor's political legacy was a mixed one. On the one hand he had provided Senegal with a degree of peace, political stability, tolerance and freedom of expression that was rare in Africa. Unlike most African leaders, he knew when and how to give up power gracefully. On the other hand, (....) though committed to democratic principles, he tended to govern in the style of a presidential monarch. By concentrating so much power in his own hands and the presidency Senghor had reduced the National Assembly to a rubber stamp for his policies and discouraged lively debate and initiative within the government. (24)

What was specific about Senghor was that he left power voluntarily on December 31, 1980, and handed it to his Prime Minister, thereby being the first Head of State in a former French colony in Sub-Saharan Africa to do that. One might suggest that Senegal owed him the political stability that was rare in Africa, even if this seemed to be guaranteed by the presence of the French military, and the involvement of France, in Senegalese politics. However, some believed that he transferred power to his Prime Minister in a state of economic and financial crisis symbolised by the Structural Adjustment Programme of the International Monetary Fund and the World Bank.

In view of his nationalistic stance, Senghor can be seen as a soft, limited and imaginary nationalist in the true meaning of the term with regards to post-colonial realities in Africa. He surely was of enormous intelligence, but a dependent light; and the Achilles heel of his version of African Nationalism in the context of African reconstruction was his ideologies that seemed to make Africa a complement to the West and that Sub-Saharan Africa could assimilate into Western cultures without altering her person, which surely was contrary to African political and socio-economic independence, hence not favourable to African reconstruction.

Chapter two

Decolonised West Africa at the crossroads?

Ghana's Independence, proclaimed on March 6, 1957 gave African Nationalism a base for anti-colonial struggle in Anglophone West Africa. Like dominoes, all the other colonies in West Africa fell after Ghana; in 1960, 17 African countries seized their liberty.[81] In Anglophone West Africa Nigeria became independent in 1960, followed by Sierra Leone in 1961, and then The Gambia in 1965.[82] The departure of the colonialists from Africa symbolised the end of direct colonial domination and exploitation, finally obtaining the freedom to administer their own political and socio-economic affairs. Independence signified liberty for these countries, but it created new challenges for them as well, and many felt that it could not be meaningful for any one State as long as the others remained under colonial domination. Nkrumah consciously pointed out during the proclamation of Ghana's Independence that his country's independence could only be meaningful if it were involved in liberating and uniting Africa. (Boahen, Tidy and Webster 383)

---

[81]Benin, Burkina Faso, Cameroon, Central African Republic, Chad, Congo, Gabon Nigeria, Ivory Coast, Madagascar, Mali, Mauritania, Niger, Senegal, Somalia, Togo, Zaire.

[82] Liberia was not formally colonised because it was agreed by Europe and the United States that the country was going to be a home for freed slaves who wanted to return to Africa, a movement promoted by the American Colonisation Society, called "Back to Africa Movement." Liberia was thus chosen as a place where freed slaves from the United States could rule themselves, and under President Monroe, land was bought there for freed slaves. The (informal) "colonization" started in 1816, and Liberia became independent in 1847. However, the country included some land held by the indigenous people before the freed slaves arrived (the Americo-Liberians or Americo-Libe). There was always tension between the two groups, and the government had been dominated by Americo-Liberians up to 1980, denying the indigenous people the right to vote before 1951. The party initially set up by the Americo-Liberians had ruled the country for 133 years. However Liberia could be considered as an American colony in the informal sense because the Americo-Liberians considered themselves as the elite, better than the indigenous people and not as part of the general populace. People from other ethnic groups were often called "natives."

The end of European colonisation in Africa was followed by the inception of a number of organisations and associations to promote cooperation, solidarity and integration for socio-economic development, of which the Organisation of African Unity was the first enterprise. After independence Africans also entered into associations with their former colonisers on the bases of solidarity and cooperation. The Commonwealth and the Francophonie are a component of these post-colonial associative institutions between former colonisers and the former colonised.

The Commonwealth existed before Africa's independence, and symbolised the autonomy of English settlers. It is a product of the British Empire, the largest in the history of modern colonisation. At the end of the Empire, it was transformed into a loose association between Britain and her former dominions and colonies. After India's independence in 1947 and subsequent membership of the Commonwealth, most African countries followed in its footsteps one by one after their independence to join the Commonwealth.

The formal institution of the Francophonie was set up a long time after the independence of the French colonies in Africa. Like the Commonwealth it has objectives defined by the relationship between the former coloniser and the former colonised. A study of the structures, roles and functioning of these organisations will give us a view of their roles in African reconstruction.

Why did leaders of the former African colonies of immediate post-independence such as Kwame Nkrumah and Leopold Sedar Senghor go into associations like the Commonwealth and the Francophonie with the former colonisers after having fought them for their freedom and independence? Is it correct to qualify what most Africans consider these organisations, as a new phase of domination or influence on former colonies by the United Kingdom and France? What are the true roles of the Commonwealth and the Francophonie in African reconstruction? To help us answer these questions, it is necessary to briefly study the histories, structures, and functioning of the Commonwealth and the Francophonie.

The Economic Community of West African States (ECOWAS) is an All-West African association amongst the various institutions in post-colonial Africa established to repair the damages caused by slavery and Colonialism, by promoting socio-economic development, peace and stability. We will also look into the structure and functioning of the ECOWAS, as well as its role in African reconstruction in the perspective of globalisation.

The Commonwealth of Nations

The origin of the Commonwealth can be traced as far back as the 19th century when in 1867 Canada became the first English colony to acquire the status of "Dominion" that enabled it to enjoy autonomy of government of equal status with Britain. Australia became a dominion in 1900, followed by New Zealand in 1907, South Africa in 1910 and the Irish Free State[83] in 1921. These dominions separately signed the Treaty of Versailles,[84] thereby becoming members of the League of Nations. As they were now sovereign States, their leaders started to meet in 1887 and agreed to continue holding meetings with Great Britain every four years, called Imperial Conferences. During the sixth Imperial Conference held in London in 1926, the Prime Ministers of Great Britain and its Sovereign Dominions adopted the Balfour Report, which considered the Dominions as:

... autonomous communities within the British Empire, equal in status, in no way subordinate one to another in any aspect of their domestic or external affairs, though united by common allegiance to the Crown, and freely associated as members of the British

---

[83] The Irish Free State, 1922-48 was formed by the Anglo-Irish treaty of December 1921, which granted dominion status, with defence safeguards, to 26 counties of the south and west of Ireland. Northern Ireland almost immediately exercised its right under the Treaty to opt out of the new state.

[84] The Treaty of Versailles was the peace settlement signed in June 1919 at Versailles Palace near Paris (hence its title) between Germany and the Allies, exactly five years after the assassination of Archduke Franz Ferdinand, one of the events that triggered the start of the war. The three most important politicians present at the Conference were David Lloyd George, Georges Clemenceau and Woodrow Wilson. The armistice signed on 11 November 1918 ended the actual fighting, but it took six months of negotiations at the Paris Peace Conference to conclude the peace treaty. Of the many provisions in the treaty, one of the most important required Germany to accept exclusive responsibility for causing the war and, under the terms of articles 231-248 (the War Guilt clauses), to disarm, make substantial territorial concessions and pay reconstruction to certain countries that had formed the Entente powers. In spite of the Treaty Germany was not pacified, conciliated nor permanently weakened. This would prove to be a factor leading to later conflicts, notably and directly the Second World War.

Commonwealth of Nations. (nationalarchives.gov.uk)

This definition of autonomy was immediately adopted by Canada, and Newfoundland (that became part of Canada in 1949). The Statute of Westminster 1931, however, reserved certain residual rights to Great Britain. Australia and New Zealand adopted the Statute in 1942 and 1947 respectively. In 1913 the University Bureau of the British Empire was founded, subsequently becoming the Association of Commonwealth Universities. The history of the Commonwealth is therefore almost as old as the British Empire itself.

World War II and the decolonisation process that affected most institutions in the world did not spare the British Commonwealth. Its structure totally changed, transforming itself into a multiracial and multicultural association of sovereign and independent States, all of which had been British dominions or colonies. India's decision to join the Commonwealth in 1949 as a republic was followed by almost all the former British colonies in West Africa. Before 1949 the criteria for membership of the British Commonwealth were described by the Balfour Report of 1926. The Declaration of London issued at the meeting of Prime Ministers of the Commonwealth in 1949 transformed the British Commonwealth into the Commonwealth of Nations,[85] becoming, since then, an association attached to the ideals of promoting "racial equality" and the "sovereignty" of its member States. It became an association of choice for the majority of former British colonies that had their Independence in the 1950s and the 1960s. Ghana, Nigeria, Sierra Leone and The Gambia became members in 1957, 1960, 1961 and 1965 respectively, immediately after their Independence. On 25th June 1965, the year The Gambia acquired Independence (the last British West African colony to obtain its Independence), the Commonwealth Secretariat was established at Marlborough House in London and Arnold Smith, a Canadian diplomat, became its first Secretary-General. The Commonwealth then transformed itself into a purely international association, and Great Britain formally lost the leadership of the association. However the British Crown has remained the Head of the Commonwealth but without any real political power since the Declaration of London in 1949.[86] The Queen of England is the Head

---

[85] 17 years after Canada became a dominion, Lord Rosebery, foreshadowing the changes to come, described the British Empire as "a Commonwealth of Nations".

of State of the United Kingdom as well as fifteen (15) sovereign States, (members of the Commonwealth), known as Commonwealth realms.[87]

Martin Kitchen, in his book entitled *The British Empire and Commonwealth: a short history* defined the Commonwealth as ... "a remarkably loose and informal alliance that has no constitution or binding rules" (15).

In the Harare Declaration, 1991, the governments of member States described it as: "...a voluntary association of sovereign independent States, each responsible for its own policies, consulting and co-operating in the interests of their peoples and in the promotion of international understanding and world peace." (thecommonwealth.org)

The Commonwealth had never formally had a permanent administrative structure. In 1965 when the Secretariat was created, a permanent structure was established to administer the Association. The Secretary General of the Commonwealth is directly responsible for communication and public affairs as well as for strategic planning and evaluation; he directs and represents the association. There are two general Under Secretaries each administering one sector, either political or economic affairs. These two important branches are separate, but the Commonwealth functions well when the two offices are in harmony, because under normal circumstances none of the two sectors could stand independently in any institution or organisation. A Commonwealth representation has been established at the Headquarters of the United Nations Organisation and other international organisations such as the World Trade Organisation and the African Union.

The real objectives of the Commonwealth have been questioned, especially by some African observers and even openly by some

---

[86] During the Conference of Prime Ministers of the Commonwealth in London in 1949, the criteria that had been established by the Declaration of Balfour to acquire membership of the Commonwealth were revised to welcome India as a Republic. The British Crown remained the symbol of the Association and its head.

[87]The 15 Commonwealth Realms in addition to the UK: are Australia, New Zealand, Canada, Jamaica, Antigua and Barbuda, Belize, Papua New Guinea, St Christopher and Nevis, St Vincent and the Grenadines, Tuvalu, Barbados, Grenada, Solomon Islands, St Lucia and The Bahamas.

African leaders, about whether Great Britain was trying to use it as a means of continuing indirect imperialist influence on its former colonies as a consolation for the loss of its empire. The Gambia, just before quitting the Commonwealth of Nations in October 2013, branded it a "neo-colonial institution." (bbc.co.uk) However, Martin Kitchen underlined that "…so many mock a high-minded statement of principles and point out the… hypocrisy of some of those who supported it, but it is important in other ways." (15) In which ways then has the Commonwealth been important? Has the Commonwealth really got the will, as stipulated in the Harare Declaration, 1991, to maintain peace and liberty, to fight against racism and oppression, and promote cooperation amongst its member States? How can African reconstruction be attached to these principles?

The Commonwealth, a loose association of 54 countries, has principles that underline the equality of its Member States and the voluntary nature of the partnership stipulated in the Singapore Declaration of Commonwealth principles of 1971 by which the leaders adhered: "… to the liberty of the individual, in equal rights for all citizens regardless of race, colour, creed or political belief, and in their inalienable right to participate by means of free and democratic political processes in framing the society in which they live." (thecommonwealth.org)

These fundamental principles were reaffirmed by Article 4 of the Declaration of Harare in 1991. Colonial domination, racial prejudice and inequality of wealth were also denounced in the Declaration. The principal objectives of the Commonwealth of Nations therefore include the promotion of democracy, material and social progress, through dialogue, discussion and especially cooperation; and of course the maintenance of peace. In the Declaration of Lusaka on Racism and Racial Prejudice in 1979, the Commonwealth of Nations showed more determination to fight against racism; to promote the principles of democracy, human rights, sustainable development, and education and technology.

It is thus utterly incorrect, considering these objectives, to categorically say that Africa is not benefiting from its membership of the Commonwealth as regards African reconstruction. The Commonwealth has contributed enormously to the fight that killed apartheid in South Africa. Under the pressure of some African leaders, the Heads of Government during their meetings constantly denounced apartheid, Imperialism and other phenomena contrary to the principles of the Association. The struggle against apartheid in the 1960s that had dominated the Commonwealth Heads of Government Meetings was strategically important to Sub-Saharan Africa.

Ghana and the other Sub-Saharan African countries joined the Commonwealth because Nkrumah and his colleagues assumed that it could serve their countries a purpose. In the immediate post-colonial era, there were observable political, economic and strategic advantages for newly independent African States to become members of organisations like the Commonwealth and the Francophonie, considering their sizes and influence. For example, Nkrumah strategically made effective use of Ghana's membership of the Commonwealth by threatening to withdraw in protest at the situation in South Africa. Also at Commonwealth Conferences African leaders achieved some success in debates, and resolutions were made particularly against apartheid. Consequently this strategy led to the exclusion of apartheid South Africa from the Commonwealth in 1961. When the country renounced its politics of segregation in 1994, and established a non-racial and democratic government, it was reintegrated into the Commonwealth. This strategic position held by Nkrumah was further manifested by Ghana's withdrawal from the Commonwealth in protest at Britain's inadequate management of the crisis in South Rhodesia (now Zimbabwe). According to Nkrumah:

> The conception of the Commonwealth was built upon the idea that it provided a bridge between peoples of all races and of all stages of development. The manner in which events in Southern Rhodesia have been handled by the United Kingdom Government has undermined and destroyed this conception. In these circumstances, and in order to preserve African unity so as to facilitate the earliest formation of a Union Government for Africa, the Government of Ghana must consider withdrawing from the Commonwealth. (Address in the National Assembly, Accra, 16 December 1965)

Honouring the unanimous decision made by the OAU Council of Ministers in Addis Ababa in December 1965, Nkrumah then broke off diplomatic ties with Britain on December 15, 1965, even though some African countries did not honour the decision to follow in Nkrumah's footstep.[88] As Ghana had broken relations with Great

Britain, Nkrumah did not participate in the Commonwealth Conference that took place in Lagos in January 1966.

The Commonwealth contributed a lot to the birth of Zimbabwe, even if the same Zimbabwe withdrew from the association in 2003 after being suspended because of disagreement between the Mugabe regime and the Commonwealth on the former's alleged lack of democracy and especially his attitude towards white farmers in Zimbabwe. The diplomatic pressure of African Member States on the white minority government in Rhodesia in the 1960s, as we have just observed with the actions led by Nkrumah, contributed to the acceleration of its Independence when it later became Zimbabwe.

When the Singapore Declaration was adopted in 1971, it gave the Commonwealth of Nations a formal code of conduct. The creation of the Commonwealth Fund for Technical Co-operation (CFTC) was a demonstration of that motivation. Through the CFTC, Member States cooperate in many domains, especially in technology, which is a crucial sector for developing countries. Accordingly, the CFTC is not encouraging aid from rich to poor countries; it is instead considered as a mechanism of mutual cooperation. Member States help one another contributing funds, staff and technical assistance. There is a will to transfer know-how developed by one Member State of the Commonwealth to the others. This fund is administered by the Secretariat of the association to avoid the relationship of dependence or ascendancy that prevails between rich and poor countries whenever aid is in question. The Technical Assistant Group TAG) created by the CFTC brings together experts in many domains such as economics, law and technology as short term consultants, especially in the economic and financial sectors in Member States. The transfer of know-how is said to be functional symbolising "real partnership" and mutual assistance.

The Export Market Development (EMD) is another programme of the Commonwealth Secretariat that puts in contact buyers and sellers from different countries to promote economic activities, notably exports, as the Brandt Report[89] stipulated. This department

---

[88] The OAU had agreed that all Member States would break relations with Britain if, by 15 December, the latter had failed to suppress the Smith rebellion.

[89] The Brandt Report was the report produced by the Independent Commission on International Development Issues, chaired by Willy Brandt (former Chancellor of West Germany) in 1980. It is considered the most comprehensive and broad based analysis of the issues of international development to date. It received much publicity

has always organised regional operations for small countries that are not as competitive as the other countries. It also encourages exports of finished products of high quality instead of raw materials, since manufacturing creates jobs and increases profits.

The older and original members of the Commonwealth: Great Britain, New Zealand, Australia and Canada have usually financed the Commonwealth Development Corporation (CDC), which through the Commonwealth Financial Assistance Plan (CFAP), established in 1960, financially helps developing countries, notably Sub-Saharan African countries; some African countries themselves contribute to this fund.

The Harare Declaration integrated new objectives in the Commonwealth, ranging from the promotion of democracy, human rights and sustainable socio-economic development. This has enabled the Commonwealth to send election observers to Member States during elections whenever they are called upon to help ensure free and fair elections in a peaceful atmosphere. The Commonwealth also helps to build the capacities of its Member States in transition especially in constitutional development. For example the Commonwealth participated in the professional training of the citizens of Zimbabwe and many other Member States to acquire the necessary skills to "effectively" administer their countries after Independence without much difficulty.

The Millbrook Commonwealth Action Programme (MCAP)[90],

---

and acceptance as the best way for governments worldwide to realistically reduce the growing economic disparity between the rich North and developing South. However just like most recommendations trying to reduce the disparity between the North and the South, the proposals were never adopted by governments due to the Cold War and a resulting lack of political will to act on these issues. The Brandt Report was updated by Dr. James B. Quilligan, in 2001 in a report entitled the "Brandt Equation"; he was the director of Brandt Commission Research, a public information agency on the Independent Commission on International Development Issues between 1980 and 1987.

[90] The Millbrook Commonwealth Action Programme on the Harare Declaration, sometimes simply referred to as Millbrook, is a policy programme of the Commonwealth of Nations, drawn on 12 November 1995 at Millbrook Resort, near Queenstown, New Zealand, at the conclusion of the fourteenth Commonwealth Heads of Government Meeting. Its objective is to implement the Harare Declaration, which set out the basic political membership criteria of the Commonwealth.

adopted during the Commonwealth Heads of Government Meeting in New Zealand in 1995 confirmed the principles of the Harare Declaration, especially concerning the promotion of Democracy and development. This led to the suspension of Nigeria between November 1995 and May 1999 because of its lack of democracy during the administration of President Saani Abacha. The Islamic Republic of Pakistan was also suspended between October 1999 and May 2004, and for the second time between November 2007 and May 2008. Zimbabwe decided to leave the Commonwealth in December 2003 for the same reason after its suspension in March 2002. Recently, the Fiji Islands who had been suspended between June 2000 and December 2001, suffered another suspension in December 2006, following a military coup. The most recent withdrawal from the Commonwealth came from The Gambia in October 2013, accusing the organisation for being a "neo-colonial institution" (bbc.com). The Gambia further said that it would "never be a member of any neo-colonial institution and will never be a party to any institution that represents an extension of Colonialism." The Commonwealth however "expressed relief that Gambia has removed itself as the country's human rights record was getting worse and worse." (sky.com)

The Commonwealth also holds a bureau of liaison in New York at the United Nations, for small countries[91] from Africa, Asia, the Pacific and the Caribbean, which otherwise might find it financially difficult to maintain a permanent presence at the United Nations. This is a positive example of Commonwealth cooperation and assistance. The smallest Member States receive assistance in the domain of technical and professional education. The Association of Commonwealth Universities[92] has established a network of higher education in its Member States. The Commonwealth Africa Investment Fund (COMAFIN) was set up in 1996 to encourage investment in 19 African countries.[93] This has helped pave the way

---

[91]The eleven small states that currently have emissaries working at the New York Office are Dominica, The Gambia (has now withdrawn), Grenada, Maldives, Nauru, St. Vincent and the Grenadines, Samoa, The Seychelles, The Solomon Islands, Tuvalu, and Vanuatu.

[92] The Association of Commonwealth Universities (about 328 universities).

[93]It has invested in agro-business and horticulture projects, mobile communications, brewery, real estate, mining and private infrastructure in Ghana, Kenya, Mozambique, South Africa, Uganda and Zambia.

for a new fund for Africa (the Pan-Commonwealth Africa Partners) launched during the 2002 CHOGM. The investment strategy of this new Fund is to find and support businesses across all industries and services to promote regional and trans-African operations. By June 2005, US $90 million had been committed by the International Finance Corporation (IFC), the Development Bank of Southern Africa and the Dutch Development Agency (FMO).[94]The Pan-Commonwealth Africa Partners Fund now stands at $103 million, supporting the expansion of existing businesses to become regional or Pan-African businesses. This accordingly helps in developing the scale and strength of business in Africa to be internationally competitive (thecommonwealth.org).

During the Commonwealth Heads of Government Meetings, Member States with different resources and capacities meet "as equals" to come to a consensus on questions that concern individual Member States or the Association collectively. They search for the means to promote good governance and socio-economic development in an atmosphere of peace and security. The Heads of Government Meeting in the Nigerian Capital, Abuja (5-8 December 2003) for example, was absorbed in a controversy over President Robert Mugabe's governance and land policy in Zimbabwe. The Commonwealth Heads of Government Meetings (CHOGM) are important as the problems confronting the Member States are discussed through "dialogue, discipline and sincerity." These discussions are vital for small countries that do not always have the chance to have their voices heard in other international gatherings. The Commonwealth Member States work as "trusted partners" for all the peoples of the Association and as a force for equality, peace, progress, prosperity, democracy, and good governance. The

---

[94] The Netherlands Development Finance Company (FMO) is the international development bank of the Netherlands. It invests risk capital in companies and financial institutions in developing countries. Its objective is to create flourishing enterprises which can serve as engines of sustainable growth. The Netherlands Development Finance Company (FMO) supports the private sector in developing countries and emerging markets in Asia and Africa as well as in Latin America and Central and Eastern Europe through loans, participations, guarantees and other investment promotion activities. Its goal is to contribute to the structural and sustainable economic growth in these countries and, together with the private sector, obtain healthy returns.

Commonwealth can therefore be considered as a global consensus building machine and a source for sustainable socio-economic development.

The Canadian government has always generously donated to the Commonwealth. Even on the issue of apartheid on which the former British dominions commented with reserve, Canada was always relatively more open. This generosity and openness of Canada was however probably due to the fact that Canada having realised that it was not playing a major international role as a world power, saw in the Commonwealth the means of becoming more prominent on the international scene.

The number of States that have joined the Commonwealth of Nations has increased enormously since its transformation in 1949. We have seen that even Mozambique which had not been colonised by Great Britain became a member. In 1956 the Commonwealth had 10 members,[95] which increased to 42 in 1981, and now it has 53 Member States after the pulling out of The Gambia in October 2013. This expansion made the association more complex, more international and culturally more diverse, seemingly symbolising its popularity and effective functioning, and the success of the British system. We have seen that some countries, which were not colonised by Britain and did not have English as their official language joined the Commonwealth. Others like Gabon, whilst not becoming member, have decided to adopt English as an official language alongside French. The diversity of the Commonwealth pushed it to assume new roles in its endeavour to promote economic and social development through good governance, education and technology.

The Commonwealth can therefore be considered as beneficial to Africa, in many domains as we have stipulated. It is however crucial to see if these benefits outweigh any disadvantage(s) that Sub-Saharan Africa's membership of the Commonwealth might breed.

The Commonwealth might abide by the principles of human rights and good governance, but the history of British colonisation would continue to weigh on it. Its members were once all British dominions and colonies, with the exception of Cameroon and Mozambique.[96] The Member States are all linked to the same

---

[95] United Kingdom, Canada, South Africa - left in 1961 but rejoined 1994; Irish Free State - left in 1949; Newfoundland - became province of Canada in 1994; Australia - invited 1931 but ratified 1942; New Zealand - invited 1931 but ratified 1947; India (1947), Pakistan (1947; left in 1972 but rejoined 1989), Sri Lanka (1948)

language, (English), most have almost the same system of law, public administration and education inherited from the former colonial master, even if some countries are now transforming their systems of government and public administration.

We have also noticed that the major part of the assistance in the Commonwealth has come principally from the old British Commonwealth. This aid was mostly considered by many observers, especially during the Cold War, as a deterrent to the influence of Communism or of the former Soviet Union on Africa, rather than as a genuine contribution to the process of sustainable development in Africa. Also the impossibility or reluctance of Great Britain to stop the racist government in Southern Rhodesia in the 1960s and the socio-political situation in apartheid South Africa drove some African countries to turn to the Soviet Union as an alternative.

The principles of the Commonwealth might genuinely be based on equality and cooperation, but Great Britain seems to always have a commanding role by default as far as the other Member States are concerned, especially its former colonies. This was confirmed by the attitude of the British Prime Minister before the Commonwealth Heads of Government Meeting in London in 1977 that coincided with the Silver Jubilee anniversary of the reign of Queen Elizabeth II. Before this meeting, the political situation in Uganda during the administration of Idi Amin Dada was the major issue facing the Commonwealth. The then Prime Minister of Britain, Lord Callaghan, informed President Amin directly that he was not welcome in England:

A statement said the Government had been alerted at the cabinet meeting that the dictator's plane was approaching Dublin airport. The Minister for Justice signed an exclusion order under the 1935 Aliens Act prohibiting Idi Amin from landing in or entering the State. Uganda radio had apparently announced that Ireland was amongst possible stopovers for Amin. A year earlier Britain had broken off diplomatic relations with his regime. Subsequently Amin declared he had beaten the British and conferred upon himself the title of CBE (Conqueror of the British Empire). British Prime Minister Jim Callaghan had made

---

96 A part of Cameroon was colonised by France, and Mozambique was colonised by Portugal.

clear he would not be welcome at the London summit. (irishabroad.com)

This direct decision of Britain through its Prime Minister put the African leaders and indeed the Association itself in a difficult position. If Britain was worried about the violation of human rights in Uganda, this unilateral decision was inappropriate, because Idi Amin Dada was not coming to Britain on a private visit. It appeared also as a violation of the basic Commonwealth principles of non-interference, in spite of the fact that the rules of the Commonwealth were never formally binding on any Member State. If according to the Commonwealth principles, Britain had the right to prevent Idi Amin from coming to England it seemed wrong to stop a Head of State of a Member State of the Commonwealth from attending a Commonwealth Heads of Government Meeting. Moreover, Britain according to the Commonwealth principles has no right to interfere, especially unilaterally, with the domestic politics of a Member State. If a solution was to be found by the Commonwealth, it concerned all its members, not only the United Kingdom. If the United Kingdom wanted to play a moral role in what was going on in Uganda, the principles of the Commonwealth disallowed her to do that without bringing the matter to the Heads of Government. The British Prime Minister's attitude towards the Ugandan President seemed to confirm Britain's dominant role or influence on the Commonwealth, which certainly evoked the solemn years of the colonial era.

The Commonwealth has also been viewed as a means of expanding the usage of the English language, which is already the dominant language today, because it is the most widely spoken in the world. It should be noted that this fact is, however, due to the economic power of the United States of America, instead of the direct influence of the British systems and institutions. However the internationalisation of the Commonwealth has also symbolised the end of the British Empire which in the 20th century lost its position as the major world power to the United States. This reality looks ironic since Great Britain seems to logically consider the Commonwealth as a consolation for the loss of its empire as well as a symbol of the success of its institutions and system. No empire in the history of colonisation had left behind it such a large network of economic, political and cultural systems as the British Empire.

It is evident that the Commonwealth has neither a constitution nor binding rules, it is a forum for discussion, and therefore not an organisation destined to take political decisions. The fact that Member States are not legally bound by Commonwealth principles and policies allows them to go against these principles especially when it concerns their domestic policies. However this seems to hamper the good functioning of the Commonwealth. For example some Member States continued to have political and cultural ties with apartheid South Africa. New Zealand continued organising sports events with South Africa in contradiction of the Gleneagles Agreement.[97]

Some people considered the Commonwealth as an association through which rich countries (former colonisers and dominions) aided poor countries (the former colonised). According to this argument, the relation of domination and dependence that has always existed between any two parties whenever aide is concerned is always present. The existence of the Commonwealth is based on a common history, either migration, (New Zealand, Australia, Canada) or colonisation, for the new Member States. All the Member States except Mozambique and a part of Cameroon have this historical link with the United Kingdom. It is the British system of politics, education and law that predominates most Member States of the Commonwealth of Nations since the most powerful Member States have all adopted the British system, which is not astonishing at all because the inhabitants of the dominions were British emigrants and had family links with Great Britain. The Commonwealth exists today simply because the British Empire existed, consequently it cannot easily be detached from Imperialism. However it would be an outright exaggeration to say that the Commonwealth has been founded on the principles of imperial exploitation.

---

[97] The Gleneagles Agreement was unanimously approved by the Commonwealth of Nations' Heads of Government at a meeting at Gleneagles, Auchterarder, Scotland in 1977. The agreement was part of their support for the international campaign against apartheid, that attempted to discourage contact and competition between their sportsmen and sporting organisations from South Africa. The Gleneagles Agreement was a reinforcement of the commitment of the Commonwealth of Nations, embodied in the Singapore Declaration of Commonwealth Principles (1971) that opposes racialism. This commitment was further strengthened by the Declaration on Racism and Racial Prejudice adopted at the Commonwealth Heads of Government Meeting in Lusaka in 1979.

Also, even if the Commonwealth has rejected all forms of domination, the mere presence of Great Britain associating with all its former colonies might raise some eyebrows. Member States have all recognised the British Crown as Head of the Association, even though the power of the British monarch is only symbolic by the fact that it exercises no political control over them. The 1930 Statute of Westminster proclaimed the Commonwealth as a free association of autonomic governments united by allegiance to the British Crown, in other words the dominions. According to the Declaration of London of 1949, new Member States, former colonies just independent, accepted the British Crown as a symbolic head of the Association.

As the years have passed, the influence of the British system within the Commonwealth has disappeared gradually except the symbolic leadership of the British monarch as Head of the Commonwealth of Nations. As the Empire belongs to the past now, there seem to be no political aspects linking the Member States of the Commonwealth to Great Britain. The importance of the role of the Secretary General of the Commonwealth, elected by the Heads of State and Government of the Commonwealth, who is responsible for the administration of the association has shown that the control that Great Britain exercised on the Commonwealth has now substantially reduced. If we observe the political situation of the two biggest and potentially richest countries in Anglophone West Africa, Nigeria and Ghana, their attachment to the British system of government did not last very long. After the instability caused by the coup d'état that overthrew the regime of Kwame Nkrumah, and the economic problems (inflation and the instability of the prices of goods and services) that has affected many "Third World" countries, Ghana returned to normalcy after the intervention of Flight Lieutenant JerryJohn Rawlings in the military coup and the elections of 1979 that put Dr Hilla Limann in power, before Rawlings seized power again on December 31, 1981, less than two years later. The new constitution adopted democracy, but the political system that it created orientated Ghana more towards Washington than London.

The two constitutions that followed in Nigeria in 1979 and 1999, when General Abdusalami Abubakar pioneered a transition towards democracy after the death of President Sani Abacha, were not different from the American style of constitution. Even the constitution of the Republic of The Gambia is not a perfect British model now. It is more orientated towards the United States of

America in spite of being based on unicameralism. The governments of these countries, after Independence adopted the Westminster model, which to a certain degree was indirectly imposed on them. The processes of democracy of the countries in Anglophone West Africa are no longer in line with the principles of Westminster. Great Britain would have surely preferred to see the British systems take a strong root in her former colonies in Africa.

The central value of the Commonwealth is an attachment to democracy, respect for individual rights and social and economic development. Its activities show that it is a modern multiracial association that plays a progressive role in this new millennium. However its nature and functioning present it as a post-colonial association that tends to draw its Member States more towards the culture and systems of Britain. This has a tendency for Africa to not consider its cultural institutions, notably the development of its languages as official or working languages. This has consequently affected Africa's cultural independence, especially concerning the development of its languages. A people's culture, particularly language, is one of the major and indispensable pillars of their socio-economic development.

L'Organisation Internationale de la Francophonie (OIF)

In 1968 during the meeting of the Heads of State of the *Organisation Commune Africaine et Malgache* (OCAM)[98], initiated by Hamani Diori of Niger, Habib Bourguiba of Tunisia, Norodom Sihanouk of Cambodia and Léopold Sédar Senghor of Senegal, the former French colonies proposed an annual conference of Francophone Heads of State. This led to the signing of the Convention that established the *Agence de Coopération Culturelle et Technique(ACCT)*,[99] in Niamey by representatives of 21States and governments on 20 March 1970. It was later transformed to the *Agence Intergouvernemental de la Francophonie* (AIF),[100] in 1998 to illustrate its international status. Finally, the adoption of a new Charter of the Francophonie in 2005 renamed the AIF, the *Organisation International de la Francophonie* (OIF).

The objectives of the ACCT were to continue cultural and mostly linguistic ties amongst its members, in order to "understand one another", and collaborate to help one another by the usage of French as a common official language. The first summit bringing together France and its former colonies took place in Paris in 1973. The Francophonie was, however, formally established and confirmed in 1986 during the first Conference of Heads of State and Government of Francophone countries, organised by President François Mittérand, in Paris.

Just like the Commonwealth, a number of observers have argued that the Francophonie, which is a product of French colonisation and created on the basis of colonial links, is an imperial instrument for France. The fact that French, a language introduced and/or imposed by France on its colonial subjects during the colonial conquest, is the catalyst and official language of the Francophonie, shows that, by its nature, it is not radically different from the Commonwealth.

The initial concept of the Francophonie was geographic, according to the inventor of the term, Onésime Reclus,[101] referring to

---

[98] Common African and Malagasy Organisation.

[99]Agency for Cultural and Technical Cooperation.

[100] The Inter-governmental Agency of the Francophonie. It is the main operator of the cultural, scientific, technical, economic and legal cooperation programmes decided at the Summits. The Agency's headquarters are in Paris and it has three regional branches in Libreville, Gabon; Lomé, Togo; and Hanoi, Vietnam.

the total number of people whose mother tongue or official language was French. The noun taken from the adjective "Francophone" characterises the populations who speak the French language. It also carries a notion of solidarity born from the sharing of "common values," especially a common language, which is what created the institutional sense of the Francophonie. When we relate the role of the Francophonie to Sub-Saharan Africa's reconstruction efforts, it is this institutional aspect we are referring to. These common values of the language and solidarity are today the principal themes, which have given birth to the *Organisation International de la Francophonie*.

The former colonies have officially used French as a medium of communication even after Independence which has left them attached to France by default. Although the Francophonie in its present institutional form, just like the Commonwealth, did not exist during colonisation, the term in its informal sense existed, as we have just said, before the independence of African countries. The two associations were formally restructured after colonisation. The most remarkable difference lies in their modern (post-colonial) versions, i.e. their present institutional forms.

It is therefore important to find out the motivations behind Léopold Sédar Senghor and his comrades' initiation of an annual conference of Francophone countries that led to the establishment of today's *Organisation International de la Francophonie*. Why did Francophone West Africans and their Anglophone counterparts not create an association amongst themselves to promote at least some of their cultures and national languages such as Kiswahili, Fulfulde, Mandenkan,[102] Hausa, Wolof in order to use them as official languages? Why have they not encouraged the Francophonie to introduce some of the African languages alongside French? Is the Francophonie really an instrument of domination of former colonies by the former colonisers as some observers have suggested? In sum what is the real function of the Francophonie? To answer these

---

[101] It was the French geographer Onésime Reclus (1837-1916) who invented the term in 1880 to designate the community of peoples that used French in their daily lives. This definition, which carries the initial sense of the *Francophonie*, only referred to geographic and cultural values; there was no political significance attached to it.

[102] Mandenkan is a term employed by the African Academy of Languages (ACALAN) to group together Bamanakan spoken in Mali, Julakan in Burkina Faso and Ivory Coast, Mandinkakan in The Gambia and Senegal and Maninkakan in Guinea (Conakry), which are varieties of the same linguistic family. The suffix, kan, means language, i.e Mandenkan means language of (the people of) Manden.

questions by exploring the motivation(s) behind this movement and objectively assessing them with regards to African reconstruction, it is necessary to study its modern structure and functioning. We have said that the *Organisation International de la Francophonie* is an international association founded on the basis of sharing common values and French as a common language. Its weight is identical to that of the Commonwealth in terms of representation; both Associations have brought together more than one quarter of the Member States of the United Nations Organisation. Xavier Deniau[103] described it as:

... a space of dialogue, cooperation and partnership with the deepest respect for its diversity. Its unity is based on a community of values of the language; dedicated to the promotion of peace, justice, security, solidarity, democracy as well as human rights and fundamental freedom that are universal and undeniable. (7)[104]

The Francophonie is a "space of dialogue, cooperation and partnership," but looking at it closely, one can observe that the respect of its cultural diversity, just like that of the Commonwealth, seemed to be compromised by the fact that its unity, according to Xavier Deniau "is based on a community of values of the language" and not the languages of its Member States. The cultural diversity of the Francophonie and the Commonwealth would have been more appropriate if some important African languages had been considered as working languages of the Association in partnership with French and English respectively.

---

[103] Xavier Deniau was former Member of the French Parliament of the Loiret and Secretary of State for French departments and overseas territories under Prime Minister Pierre Messmer from 5th July 1972 to 28th March 1973. He played a fundamental role in the Francophonie as Secretary General of the International Association of Parliamentarians of the French Language - *l'Association International des Parlementaires de Langue Française (AIPLF)*, now Parliamentary Assembly of the Francophonie.

[104]...un espace de dialogue, de coopération et de partenariat dans le plus profond respect de sa diversité. Son unité se fonde sur une communauté de valeurs de la langue; consacrée à la promotion de la paix, de la justice, de la sécurité, de la solidarité, de la démocratie ainsi qu'au respect des droits de l'homme et des libertés fondamentales, qui sont universels et indéniables.

The structure of the Francophonie consists principally of the Conference of Heads of State and Government, which since 1986 has been called "Summit," and has periodically brought together the Heads of State and Government of Member States. It is the highest gathering of the Francophonie, and defines its direction in such a way to assure its influence in international relations as a means of fulfilling its objectives. During each meeting the delegates dialogue in discipline and adopt projects and programmes for the two years following the summit. It is presided over by the Head of State or Government of the host country up to the next summit. We have said that the first Francophone summit was organised in France in 1986, and it brought together 41 States. The three priority sectors discussed by the representatives during this meeting were cultural industry, language, scientific information and the development of technology including research.

The second structure of the Francophonie is the *Conférence Ministériel de la Francophonie* (CMF)[105], which is held between summits and in which the Member States are represented by their Foreign Affairs ministers or the ministers responsible for Francophone affairs. The ministerial conference has the task of implementing the decisions made during the last summit and to prepare the next summit as a means of assuring the continuity of the organisation; the admission of new members is recommended by the Ministerial Conference.

The Permanent Council[106] is another organ of the Francophonie and its principal agent, acting on behalf of the Inter-governmental Agency of the Francophonie, and other direct operators like the Agency of Francophone Universities, TV5,[107] the Senghor University of Alexandria and the *Association internationale des maires et responsables des capitales et métropoles partiellement ou entièrement francophones (AIMF)[108]*a s well as the *Assemblée parlementaire de la Francophonie (APF)*.[109] Finally

---

[105]Ministerial Conference of the Francophonie

[106] The Permanent Council of the Francophonie consists of Ambassadors of the Member States, and, like the ministers' conferences, its main task is to plan future summits and also to supervise the implementation of summit decisions on a day-to-day basis.

[107] An international French-speaking television network.

[108]International Association of Mayors and Officials of Partially or Wholly Francophone Capitals and Major Cities

[109]The Parliamentary Assembly of the Francophonie. It created in Luxembourg in

there is the *Haut conseil de la Francophonie,*[110] a structure created on 19 January 2004originally under the name of *Conseil consultatif de la francophonie,*[111]placed under the Secretary General. It is responsible for studying the major trends of the evolution and future of the organisation, both medium and longterm, a task which makes it a think tank for the Francophonie. The Executive Secretariat of the Francophonie is administered by the Secretary General, elected during the Summit as stipulated in the Charter. The Secretary General of the Francophonie, who is its spokesperson and official representative of its political actions, leads the organisation and serves as the basis of its institutional apparatus. The Secretary General facilitates multilateral cooperation, ensures the harmonious working of the programmes and activities of all operating agencies, and proposes priority domains for multilateral actions. The four-year mandate of Secretary General is carried out under the authority of the three main institutions of the Francophonie, namely, the Summit, the Ministerial Conference and the Permanent Council.

The initial objective of the International Organisation of the Francophonie was, as we have noted, principally the pursuit of linguistic and cultural ties with France. Taking into account its origin, one cannot qualify it as an exclusively political association, but considering the nature of its evolution since its inception and in particular since the Hanoi summit of 1997, we cannot either detach it completely from the sphere of politics. However, some consider that the Francophonie is political "…only in the sense that it is preoccupied with the interest of the Francophone space." (Deniau 6)[112] Like the Commonwealth, it has principles and outlined new objectives which were proposed at the Cotonou summit in December 1995. By the will of the Heads of State and Government of Member States, during the Hanoi summit in November 1997, the Francophonie was transformed into an international political and multicultural institution, symbolised by the creation of a Secretariat.

1967, and was given the status of Consultative Assembly of the Francophonie [*Assemblée consultative de la Francophonie*] at the Mauritius Summit in 1993. Consequently, it takes part in Summit proceedings, as well as those of the Ministerial Conferences and the Permanent Council dealing with specific subjects.

[110]High Council of the Francophonie

[111]Consultative Council of the Francophonie.

[112]…*qu'au sens où elle se préoccupe des intérêts de la "cité francophone".*

The adoption of that Charter gave the Francophonie a political face, ceasing to exist exclusively as an association of cultural exchange based on the practice of the French language. The Francophonie helps:

> ...to install and develop democracy, to prevent conflict and promote the rule of law and Human Rights, intensify dialogue of cultures and civilisations, bring together people by their mutual knowledge reinforcing their solidarity through multilateral cooperation in view of favouring economic development.(Article 1)[113]

Following the 1986 Conference, biennial summits have taken place, during which the Heads of State and Government discuss matters relating to the objectives of the Organisation. The role of the Secretary General consists of endeavouring to have the Francophonie evolve to a more politically active force, capable of playing an important role on the international scene. During the Ouagadougou summit in November 2004, the Declaration intended to transform the Francophonie to "...a zone of solidarity for sustainable development." The Inter-governmental Agency of the Francophonie, that is the principal operator of the cultural, economic, jurisdictional, scientific and technical programmes of the Francophonie, encourages and assures the promotion of new technologies for development. It helps Member States to build and extend the rule of law and democracy. Secondly the question of education has ever been important in the Francophonie and during the first conference organised by a Sub-Saharan African Head of State (President Abdou Diouf of Senegal who has been the Secretary General of the Association since 2003), the participants focused the major part of their work on education in Member States. Education and training are vital to all forms of sustainable development, and the level of education in Africa having been considered inferior to that in Europe, the African continent should under normal circumstances benefit from its cooperation with France and the other Member States in terms of education. Consequently the Senghor University of Alexandria was instituted at the Dakar Summit in 1989, and opened

---

[113]...à l'instauration et au développement de la démocratie, à la prévention des conflits et au soutien à l'État de droit et aux droits de l'Homme; à l'intensification du dialogue des cultures et des civilisations ; au rapprochement des peuples par leur connaissance mutuelle ; au renforcement de leur solidarité par des actions de coopération multilatérale en vue de favoriser l'essor de leurs économies.

in 1990. This University is a private institution of higher education of an international standing to contribute to the promotion of development, particularly in Africa. A number of students are being trained in the field of administration, management and public health, and cultural patrimony. The University's contribution to African reconstruction cannot be underestimated or neglected. It carries the name of Léopold Sédar Senghor, one of the most memorable and "assimilated" personalities of all the founding fathers of the Francophonie of today. The paradox however is that teaching in this university established to also reflect the realities of African development, is done exclusively in French. The University should have introduced into its curriculum some African cultures and languages like Kiswahili, Hausa, Lingala, Wolof, Mandenkan which are as rich and resourceful as the French language, and are inevitable catalysts of development in Africa.

The introduction of the two dominant foreign languages in West Africa, (English and French), started with commerce in the 18th century, when French trading posts were established in Senegal, but their expansion took place through military conquest. If the use of these languages by Sub-Saharan African countries was not formally obligatory after independence, it was neither voluntary in the formal sense. African leaders automatically chose them as their official languages to effectively communicate with the wider world, in the administration of their respective governments, because they were said to be the most "viable" alternatives. In the immediate post-colonial period, they appeared to be indispensable and less menacing, in the short term, in the face of the multiplicity of African languages, and the rivalry of some tribal groups. This situation was however not a simple occurrence; it was largely generated by the divide and rule tactic of Colonialism. For example, the colonisers ingeniously and strategically favoured some tribal groups and their languages over others, generating friction to the point of enmity amongst the peoples of the same countries in Africa. Most civil conflicts and wars, for example the Rwandan genocide, germinated from this phenomenon.

If we take Senegal and the Gambia as an example, these countries were not geographically demarcated as they are today at the level of administration such as the colonisers had established after the Berlin Conference and the colonial conquest that followed it. They had only been divided into kingdoms of Mandingoes, Wolofs, Toukoulors…, and had been administered by the tribes in the different regions. In these kingdoms dismantled by the European colonisers during the colonial conquest, several distinct tribes had dwelled. It was logically the languages of the tribes in each kingdom that were used in the territories. Colonisation strategically destroyed this natural cultural trend causing civil strife.

If the French language is used today as the official language in France, it is simply because it was the language of the King of France. In France the diffusion of French preoccupied the monarchy from the 16th century, a period when French was in direct competition with Latin and other dialects. The same observation could be applied to the history of Spanish, Arabic, English, Portuguese... William the Conqueror's invasion of England in 1066 largely removed the native ruling class and replaced it with a foreign, French-speaking monarchy, aristocracy and clerical hierarchy. Norman French which was the language of the conqueror became the language of administration and the courts, hence the official language.[114] But the fact that Western colonisation regrouped different tribes in different regions of Africa and separated others that had been in the same geographic regions or kingdoms haphazardly, according to the strategic interests of the colonisers, made it impossible for the languages of the colonised to any more cover their regions or kingdoms; in fact most kingdoms were dismantled during the conquest. The inevitable result of this colonial policy turned these multiple languages into rivalry and created conflict.

We have said that the French language as a common language in the Francophonie existed well before the formal inception of the Organisation. But the formalisation of the *Organisation International de la Francophonie that strategically oc*curred alongside decolonisation has

[114] The Norman Conquest introduced Anglo-Norman, a northern dialect of Old French, as the language of the ruling classes in England, displacing Old English. This was strengthened in the mid-twelfth century by an influx of the followers of the Angev in dynasty (the residents of Anjou, a former province of the King of France, as well as the residents of Angers), who spoke a more mainstream dialect of French. It was only in the fourteenth century that English regained its former primacy, but the use of French at court continued into the fifteenth century. By this time English was profoundly transformed, developing into the different Middle English which formed the basis for the modern language. A large proportion of English words were replaced by French words, during the centuries of French linguistic dominance, leading to the present hybrid of English vocabulary combined with a largely French abstract vocabulary.

solidified the use of French especially in former French colonies. This has had the tendency of denying Sub-Saharan Africans the possibility of promoting and developing their languages so as to use them in partnership with French as official languages. Of course French and English have kept Africa in touch with the wider world in the field of commerce and administration. President Senghor during a speech he delivered in Congo Kinshasa (today Zaire) in 1969 declared that the French language:

> …is for us a precious means of communication with the exterior and to know others as ourselves. The Francophonie is an endless humane will without limit that stretches towards a synthesis always overtaking itself to better adapt to the situation of a perpetually changing world …(qtd. in Deniau 20)[115]

According to some observers, the position of France as a former colonial power, and that of Sub-Saharan African countries as former colonies confirms the point that the Francophonie has been an instrument to reset French influence on the former French colonies; the same accusation has been levelled at the Commonwealth. Accordingly, the creation of a permanent secretariat of the Francophonie in 1997, based in Paris and that of the Commonwealth of Nations in London further supported this idea. In fact the Francophonie, according to the words of Léopold Sédar Senghor, is nothing but "a Commonwealth in the French style."[116] (Ibid)

The priority attached to the promotion of the French language in international relations is distinctly a subject that all the French political parties agreed on. Since the first summit was held, French governments have supported the Francophonie and promoted the French language to the point of creating a Ministry of the Francophonie, just like Britain's Foreign and Commonwealth Office.[117]

---

[115] … pour nous un moyen précieux de communication avec l'extérieur et de connaissance des autres comme de nous-mêmes. La francophonie est une volonté humaine sans cesse tendue vers une synthèse et toujours en dépassement d'elle-même pour mieux s'adapter à la situation d'un monde en perpétuel devenir.

[116] …à la française

[117] The Foreign and Commonwealth Office is headed by the Secretary of State for Foreign and Commonwealth Affairs, simply referred to as the Foreign Secretary. The position of Secretary of State for Foreign and Commonwealth Affairs came into existence in 1968 with the merger of the functions of Secretary of State for Foreign

As far back as in 1926, at the peak of colonisation, writers in the French language created the *Association des écrivains de langue française* (Adelf).[118] They were followed in 1950, still in the period of colonisation, by journalists using the French language as a medium, to establish the *Union internationale des journalistes et de la presse de langue française*,[119] which has now become the *Union de la Presse francophone*.[120] A Francophone Community Radiowas launched in 1955, withpublic *Radio France*, *Radio Belge Francophone*, *Radio Canada* and *Radio Suisse Romande*. This Francophone Community Radio today offers, with a constantly growing audience, common simulcasts on member radiowaves, thus contributing to the strengthening of the French language and the Francophone community at large.

The first Francophone intergovernmental institution was born when the *Conférence des Ministres de l'Education* (Confemen)[121] was organised in 1960, in which fifteen (15) countries participated. This Ministerial conference is now permanent and takes place every two years to draw the guidelines on education and training in the forty-one (41) Member States and Governments. Universities got involved, creating one year later the *Association des universités partiellement ou entièrement de langue française*,[122] which in 1999 was transformed to the *Agence Universitaire de la Francophonie (AUF)*.[123] It is one of the specialised operators of the Francophonie and now has 677 higher education and research institutions in 81 countries. (francophonie.org) Other organisations at administrative level followed, such as the creation of the *Haut Comité pour la défense et l'expansion de la langue française*[124] in 1966 by Georges Pompidou, which in 1973 became the *Haut Comité de la langue française*.[125]

The parliamentarians in their turn launched their international association in 1967, becoming the *Assemblée Parlementaire de la Francophonie* (APF)[126] in 1997. It brings together 65 members and 11

Affairs and Secretary of State for Commonwealth Affairs into a single Department of State.

[118] Association of Writers of the French Language.

[119] International Union of Journalists and the French press.

[120] Union of Francophone Press.

[121] Conference of Ministers of Education.

[122] The Association of Partially or Wholly French-language universities.

[123] University Agency of the Francophonie.

[124] High Commission for the Defence and the Expansion of the French language

[125] High Commission for the French language

[126] Parliamentary Assembly of the Francophonie (APF).

observers and represents the Consultative Assembly of the Francophonie institutional framework according to the Charter of the Organisation. The *Conference des ministres de la Jeunesse et des Sports* (Conféjes),[127] created in 1969, is the second permanent Ministerial Conference of the Francophonie.

Initially then, the promotion of the French language and culture was the primary mission of the Francophonie, before the promotion of cultural and/or linguistic diversity. Even the *Conférence des ministres de l'Éducation nationale des pays d'expression française* (CONFEMEN),[128] whose objective is to encourage cooperation and coordination in the domain of education policies, and to take high-level discussions on the future of education, initially operated exclusively around the French language.

This linguistic feature proper to the Francophonie is symbolised by the fact that the status of membership was initially linked to the condition that French must be the official language, the second official language, or be used in teaching in the country that desired to be a member. However since the summit of Mauritius Island in 1993, the restriction on membership status of the Francophonie was lifted. Some countries which were not colonised by France and do not have French as their official language are now members of the *Organisation International de la Francophonie*, for example Romania whose official language is Romanian, and Bulgaria, official language, Bulgarian. In 1995, Guinea Bissau and St. Thomas & Prince (official language, Portuguese,) became members. The Francophonie or France might have realised that the policy of almost conditioning States interested in becoming members of the Organisation to take up French as their official language or to introduce it in their curricula had not been very successful, and that the more there were countries joining the Francophonie, the more its systems, values and culture including the language would be shared and promoted, which would logically have both political and socio-economic advantages in the long term.

Another demonstration of the insistence on the French language in the Francophonie was the launching of the international television channel TV5 in 1984. This was a direct operator of the Francophonie in the field of communication and the media. It was the first

---

[127] Conference of Ministers of Youth and Sports.
[128]Conference of Education Ministers of French-speaking Countries

international TV station that broadcast its programmes exclusively in French. In a world where the English language remains progressively the number one international language, it is unsurprising, in this era of Anglo-Saxon hegemony, that France looks for a means of promoting its language beyond the Francophone community, to try to regain more influence following the loss of its empire. The national or local languages of the other former colonial powers went beyond their frontiers, but very few of these countries have demonstrated such a vigour and determination as France to propel its language beyond its frontier and to seemingly use it as a vector to re-establish its influence in the world, especially in its former colonies. Indeed France had considered herself as a carrier of a cultural enlightenment through its language according to the declarations of two of its former presidents, Charles de Gaulle and Georges Pompidou respectively:

> Because it is true that France has all the time laboured with passion the field of intelligence and offered to the whole world enough precious harvest, it is true that it provides the whole world a language adapted by excellence to the universal character of thought. (Deniau 22)

> Language is a privileged instrument of expression and communication amongst men, an open and generous irreplaceable support of humanism (…). The role of language is not a simple means of expression, it is a means of intellectual influence; it is by our language that we exist in the world other than a country amongst others. (ibid)[129]

If according to these propositions, the French language is "adapted by excellence to the universal character of thought" and if it is by its language that a nation exists, Africans who abandon their national languages to exclusively adopt French or English or Portuguese or Spanish, either voluntarily or involuntarily, are destroying their own identities as well as the existence of their nations.

It is difficult for both the Francophonie and the Commonwealth to escape from the accusation of linguistic Imperialism thrown at

---

[129]*Car il est vrai que la France a de tout temps labouré avec passion les champs de l'intelligence et offert à la terre entière d'assez précieuse récoltes, il est vrai qu'elle met à la disposition de tout le monde une langue adaptée par excellence au caractère universel de la pensée.*
La langue est un instrument privilégié d'expression et de communication entre les hommes, un support irremplaçable d'humanisme ouvert et généreux (…). Le rôle de la langue n'est pas un simple moyen d'expression, c'est un moyen d'influence intellectuelle ; c'est à travers notre langue que nous existons dans le monde autrement qu'un pays parmi d'autres.

them, because both associations have carried out their activities exclusively using French and English respectively as media of communication to the detriment of African languages. The difference, however, is that the United Kingdom does not seem to use the Commonwealth as an instrument to promote or popularise the use of the English language to a level that France used the Francophonie to disseminate the French language. This is most probably due to the fact that the promotion of English is guaranteed, as we have seen, by the existence and economic power of the United States of America.

Following independence, the African continent has been confronted with a number of problems. We have noticed that the protagonists of the struggle for African independence were able to effectively fight the colonial system thanks partly to their training in North America and Europe and partly to the adoption and usage of the colonisers' languages. The usage of the colonisers' languages was therefore enormously advantageous to African Nationalism. But the exclusive usage of these languages as official languages has been to the detriment of African languages especially in the post-colonial era, and has had a negative impact on cultural Nationalism and reconstruction in Africa. The effect of Africans associating with their former coloniser in the Francophonie and the Commonwealth concerns African civilisation that had existed in its oral specificity well before the slave trade and colonisation. This has consequently disappeared slowly because most African cultural values, especially languages, have been undermined by slavery, colonisation and post-colonial associations like the Commonwealth and the Francophonie. African leaders who initiated associations with these two main former colonial powers, especially in the domain of culture without advocating for their cultural values especially languages, had not constructively analysed and interpreted African realities in the light of scientific and cultural theories of the West. President Senghor declared that: "French has allured us with its abstract words that are rare in our maternal languages [...]. Each of its words is naturally surrounded by a halo of sap and blood. French words radiate with a thousand fires like rockets that enlighten our nights." (Deniau 19)[130]

---

[130]*Le français nous a séduits de ces mots abstraits et rares dans nos langues maternelles, ... Chacun des mots est naturellement nimbé d'un halo de sève et de sang. Les mots français rayonnent de mille*

Here, President Senghor is bluntly and incorrectly showing the superiority of the French language to African languages, which technically supposed that African languages are comparatively inferior. The Francophonie and the Commonwealth encourage the extension of socio-economic relations that seem to be based on partnership. If we take into account the history of European Colonialism in Africa and the economic situation of the African continent today, an extension of any other relationship between Europe and Africa without sincerity, social justice and the self-respect of Africans, can hardly escape a notion of dependence and domination. F. and B. Constantin considered African Independence as a myth which Africans cannot break:

... the relational networks that articulated their resources, their defence, their training, even some aspects of their ideology and their culture, with the ancient metropolis. In different forms the Francophonie and the Commonwealth express durably the continuity of vertical systems of privileged relation of which the structure maintained by unequal exchanges of resources equally necessary, concretised a strong relationship of domination in the form of clientelism. (59)[131]

During colonisation, the relationship between the colonisers and the colonised represented total domination in an atmosphere marked by superiority of the former and inferiority of the latter. F. and B. Constantin's critique reasonably confirms the continuity of the pre-Independence Euro-African relationship. Post-Colonialism has hampered the relationship, leading to its strategic transformation that inculcates the notion of partnership instead of the colonial aspects of domination and exploitation. The United Kingdom and France have therefore been accused of trying to extend the relationship that

---

feux comme des fusées qui éclairent notre nuit.

[131] ...les réseaux relationnels qui articulaient leurs ressources, leur défense, leur formation, sinon même certains aspects de leur idéologie et leur culture, avec l'ancienne métropole. Sous des formes différentes, l'ensemble franco-africain et le Commonwealth ont exprimé durablement cette continuité de systèmes verticaux de relations privilégiées dont la structure entretenue par les échanges inégalitaires de ressources également nécessaires, concrétisait une relation de domination élargie et dense de type clientéliste.

existed between Europe and Africa during colonisation on the pretext of partnership and cooperation. The Francophonie could be regarded as a nostalgic materialisation of French Imperialism in this post-colonial era, an imitation of the Commonwealth which also is a nostalgic materialisation of British Imperialism. Through the Francophonie and the Commonwealth, France and the United Kingdom have consolidated their influence on their former colonies in Africa, which appears to have affected African civilisation almost in the same way as Colonialism, even though it is the Africans who co-opted the Francophonie. The Francophonie in its previous form and function was incompatible with cultural Nationalism in Africa, since its doctrine and policies were based on the internationalisation of the usage of the French language. It looked more like an instrument to propagate the French language than for cultural diversity of its members.

However the Francophonie and the Commonwealth seemed to have learnt the lesson about the African Cultural Renaissance, formally initiated by President Thabo Mbeki of South Africa, and now taken up by the African Union. The Khartoum Decision of the African Union, 2006, that linked culture and education in Africa adopted the statutes of the African Academy of Languages (ACALAN) initiated by Alpha Oumar Konaré, former President of Mali and former Chairperson of the African Union Commission. Through the ACALAN, African leaders have reiterated their awareness of the roles played by African cultures and languages in African integration and development. The fact that the Francophonie and the Commonwealth are now supporting the ACALAN in its effort to promote and develop African languages as partner languages of French, English, Portuguese… is an encouraging sign for cultural diversity within the organisations and cultural Nationalism in Africa. It also gives more credit to the Francophonie and the Commonwealth in the sense that it makes them more democratically multicultural. Africa needs her own languages as well for her own development, simply because no development is appropriate if the people concerned by this process of development use other peoples' language as the main means of communication instead of the languages the majority of the population understand. African languages need to be empowered and be used in partnership with other languages such as English and French. The African Union has realised that language is a major catalyst of development as symbolised by the Khartoum Decision.

For the newly liberated countries which had fought so hard for their liberation, political independence should have been synonymous with economic and cultural independence. Adopting French and English, and failing to try to develop some of their own languages as official languages, has therefore had repercussions on the development of these languages, and consequently on their reconstruction efforts. African cultures and languages are also carriers of civilisation, and can be adapted to the universal character of thought. Africans surely benefit from their membership of the Commonwealth and the Francophonie; however these benefits can in no way compensate for the loss of identity and of African cultural and linguistic values. Simply, one cannot effectively exchange cultural values against material gains. One of the most important cultural identities of a people is their language, which is at the core of their process of development as a component of culture.

The Economic Community of West African States (ECOWAS).

The idea of African Unity as a mechanism of African reconstruction, pioneered by Dr Kwame Nkrumah and his compatriots, gave birth to the Organisation of African Unity (OAU) in 1963. As the years passed other organisations aiming at economic integration were instituted in different regions of Africa. Amongst these regional institutions shaped in post-colonial Africa was the Economic Community of West African States (ECOWAS).

The roots of the ECOWAS go far back to 1964, when President William Tubman of Liberia proposed the idea of creating a West African community. The following year, 1965, four West African countries, two Anglophone (Liberia and Sierra Leone), and two Francophone countries (Guinea and Côte d'Ivoire), signed an agreement amongst themselves, but without really creating any form of community. Seven years later, in 1972, Generals Yakoub Gowon of Nigeria and Gnassingbé Eyadéma of Togo expressed the idea again and convinced their counterparts to institute an Economic Community in West Africa. After a series of preliminary meetings in 1973, 1974 and early 1975 in Lomé, Accra and Monrovia respectively, the ECOWAS was created.

The distinctiveness of this Community, created on May 28, 1975 by the Charter of Lagos, compared to other associations such as the Commonwealth and the Francophonie, is that it was founded on purely economic grounds. Like the African Union, it is an all-African institution that aims at promoting economic development in the region. It has also, so far, partially managed to evade the colonial cultural divide of languages and public administration in the Member States of the community.

The treaty that established the Economic Community of West African States (ECOWAS) was signed by fifteen (15) West African States to attain economic cooperation and integration amongst the people of West Africa. Cape Verde became the sixteenth Member State of the Community immediately after its inception, in 1976. However, Mauritania withdrew in 2002, because of its disagreement on "community policies," thereby reducing the ECOWAS membership to fifteen (15). The community has now eight

119

Francophone Member States,[132] five Anglophone[133] and two Lusophone countries.[134]

To appraise the degree of achievement of the ECOWAS and its impact on African reconstruction especially in the West African region, in the form of sustainable socio-economic development, we have to take into account its objectives and functioning, as well as its political and military impact on governance and peacekeeping, which has now become an increasingly greater facet of its programme of activities due to the multitude of conflicts in the Community.

According to the Revised Treaty of ECOWAS, 1993, its main objective is:

...to promote co-operation and integration, leading to the establishment of an economic union in West Africa in order to raise the living standards of its peoples, and to maintain and enhance economic stability, foster relations among Member States and contribute to the progress and development of the African Continent.(article 3)

To realise these objectives, the Member States have chosen common economic resolutions. The Treaty also defined the attachment of Member States to the following fundamental principles:

...equality and inter-dependence; solidarity and collective self-reliance; inter-State co-operation, harmonisation of policies and integration of programmes; non-aggression between Member States; maintenance of regional peace, stability and security...; peaceful settlement of disputes...; recognition, promotion and protection of human and peoples' rights in accordance with the provisions of the African Charter on Human and Peoples' Rights; accountability, economic and social justice and popular participation in development; ... promotion and consolidation of a democratic system of governance...; and equitable and just distribution of the costs and benefits of economic co-operation and integration. (article 4)

---

[132] Dahomey (Benin since 1975), Upper Volta (Burkina Faso since 1984), Ivory Coast, Guinea, Mali, Niger, Senegal and Togo.

[133] The Gambia, Ghana, Liberia, Nigeria and Sierra Leone.

[134] Cape Verde, Guinea-Bissau.

The aim of the new treaty was discernibly to give teeth to the project of economic integration and development that envisaged economic and monetary union, as well as a strong political co-operation amongst the ECOWAS Member States.

The ECOWAS is a pioneering association because before its inception, African nationalists had, since Independence, concentrated more on political integration at the expense of the economy. However, the Community is not only about economic integration, it also deals, as we have just noted, with a variety of domains. The state of political instability in the West African region incited the ECOWAS to adopt a protocol on Non-aggression in Lagos, in 1978, which essentially provided for peaceful resolution of disputes in Member States. The Non-aggression protocol was followed by a relatively more elaborate protocol on Mutual Assistance on Defence (MAD), signed in Freetown in 1981, and in July 1991, Declaration A/DCL.1/7/91 on Political Principles was signed in Abuja. In 2001, Protocol A/SP1/12/01 on Democracy and Good Governance, which was Supplementary to a previous protocol signed in 1999, relating to the Mechanism for Conflict Prevention, Management, Resolution, Peacekeeping and Security was signed.

For the security of its Member States, the Authority of Heads of State and Government created the ECOMOG[135] in 1990, whose intervention for peacekeeping was operationalised at the Liberian bloody civil conflict in August 1991, with eleven (11) ECOWAS member states contributing soldiers to the ECOMOG, as well as Uganda and Tanzania.

The mechanism for conflict resolution of the ECOWAS therefore provides a framework for intervention in the region in the event of inter and intra State armed conflict in the Community with the ECOMOG as the intervention force.It has contributed to putting an end to major intra-community conflicts, especially in Guinea Bissau, Sierra Leone, Liberia and Ivory Coast.

---

[135]The Economic Community of West African States Monitoring Observer Group. It was a formal arrangement for separate armed forces to work together as an army of intervention in conflicts in Member States. The Nigerian army was its main pillar and the major part of its financial source, with army units contributed by other ECOWAS members.

The 1975 Treaty had provided for the following institutions of the Community: the Authority of Heads of State and Government; the Council of Ministers; the Executive Secretariat; the Tribunal of the Community; and Technical and Specialised Commissions, namely the:

i. Trade, Customs, Immigration, Monetary and Payments Commission,
ii. Industry, Agriculture and Natural Resources Commission,
iii. Transport, Telecommunication and Energy Commission, and
iv. Social and Cultural Affairs Commission.

When the Treaty was revised in 1993, the institution of the Tribunal of the Community was replaced by the Community Court of Justice. The new treaty established new institutions such as the Community Parliament, the Economic and Social Council and the Fund for Co-operation, Compensation and Development. The second institutional reform[136] of the ECOWAS in 2007, transformed the Executive Secretariat into the ECOWAS Commission, headed by a President.

The revision of the 1975 Treaty and the subsequent institutional reform of 2007 were motivated by a number of events, in and outside the region that required restructuring the strategies and approaches of the ECOWAS in view of transforming it into a more authentic instrument of regional economic growth and integration. The Revised Treaty, 1993, has thus geared towards extending economic and political co-operation and integration among Member States; it identified the accomplishment of a common market and a single common currency as economic objectives. In the political domain it has provided for a West African parliament, and the ECOWAS Community Court of Justice to replace the existing Tribunal as a means of effectively enforcing Community decisions, and an Economic and Social Council. The treaty has also put more emphasis on preventing and settling regional conflicts.

The Authority of Heads of State and Government of the ECOWAS, which composes of Heads of State and/or Government of Member States, is the supreme authority of the Community. It determines the major guidelines and policies by embarking on measures to ensure its development and the realisation of its

---

[136] The first reform was in 1993 when the Treaty was revised in July 1993.

objectives. The Authority also prepares and adopts its own "Rules of Procedure," and appoints the President of the Commission in accordance with the provisions of the Treaty. It also appoints the External Auditors on the recommendation of the Council. (article 7) The Authority meets once a year at least in ordinary session. An extraordinary session may be convened by the Chairperson of the Authority or at the request of a Member State on condition that such a request is supported by a simple majority of the Member States. (article 8)

The Council of Ministers comprises the Minister in charge of the ECOWAS Affairs or any other Minister designated by a Member State. The Council is responsible for the functioning and development of the Community. (article 10) It therefore, makes recommendations to the Authority of Heads of State and Government on actions and strategies according to the objectives of the Community. The Council prepares and adopts the rules of procedure of the Community; it also adopts the Staff Regulations, approves the structure, the budgets and work programmes of the Community and its institutions. (ibid) The Council of Ministers meets at least biannually in ordinary session. One of the two sessions usually immediately proceeds the ordinary session of the Authority of Heads of State and Government. The Chairperson of the Council may convene an extraordinary session at the request of a Member State supported by a simple majority. (article 11)

The President of the Commission, who is appointed by the Authority of Heads of State and Government for a four (4) year term renewable once, is the legal representative of all the institutions of the Community and the Chief Executive Officer of the Commission. The President coordinates the activities of all the institutions of the Community, represents the ECOWAS in its international relations and takes care of policy analysis, strategic planning and regional integration activities. A Vice President, who is also appointed for a mandate of four (4) years and accompanied by seven (7) Commissioners, assists the President. The role of the Vice President is to ensure the organisational continuity of the Community, especially in the absence of the President. The Vice President therefore supports the President in the exercise of duties related to the mandate of the ECOWAS. The Vice President also monitors, coordinates, and evaluates programmes, and relations between the

Commission and other ECOWAS institutions. The Vice President supervises the Community Computer Center and discharges other duties conferred by the President of the Commission.

As the Assembly of the peoples of the Community, the House of Representatives is the Parliament of the ECOWAS. It is equally known as the Community Parliament and is located in Abuja, Nigeria. The ECOWAS Parliament is a forum for dialogue, consensus building and consultation as a factor of enhancing integration. Members of the Parliament are drawn from the national parliaments of each Member State; therefore members who lose their seats in the national parliament also lose their ECOWAS Parliamentary seat. Presently the Parliament only plays a consultative and advisory role without legislative powers; its members, as we have seen, are not elected directly. The Parliament comprises one hundred and fifteen (115) seats, with each Member State having a minimum of five seats. The remaining forty (40) seats are shared according to the populations of Member States. The Revised Treaty, 1993, stipulates that the number and distribution of parliamentary seats could be reviewed by the Authority on its own initiative or upon the recommendation of the Parliament.

Representation for each Member States as follows:

No	Name of country	Seats
01	Benin	Five (5)
02	Burkina Faso	Six (6)
03	Cape Verde	Five (5)
04	Cote d'Ivoire	Seven (7)
05	The Gambia	Five (5)
06	Ghana	Eight (8)
07	Guinea	Six (6)
08	Guinea Bissau	Five (5)
09	Liberia	Five (5)
10	Mali	Six (6)
11	Niger	Six (6)
12	Nigeria	Thirty five (35)
13	Senegal	Six (6)
14	Sierra Leone	Five (5)
15	Togo	Five (5)

The ECOWAS Community Court of Justice, also created by the

1993 Revised Treaty, is the judicial organ of the Community, mandated to resolve disputes related to the Treaty of ECOWAS, protocols and conventions, by addressing complaints from Member States and institutions of the Community; it equally addresses issues relating to defaulting Member States. The Community Court alsohas competence to hear individual complaints of alleged human rights violations. Its offices are established in the Nigerian capital, Abuja. In 2005, the Supplementary Protocol A/SP.1/01/05, gave the Court jurisdiction to rule on cases of violations of human rights in any Member States. Protocol A/SP1/12/01 on Democracy and Good Governance provides that the Court hears inter alia, cases relating to violations of human rights.

The Economic and Social Council of the Community plays an advisory role on economic and social matters and includes representatives of the various categories of economic and social activity.

The ECOWAS Fund for Cooperation, Compensation and Development provided by article 21 of the 1993 Revised Treaty, gives compensation and related forms of assistance to Member States which have incurred losses as a result of the application of the provisions of the Treaty. The fund also provides loans and grants to finance national or community research and development activities, and promote development projects in the relatively less developed Member States of the Community.

The Specialised Technical Commissions of the ECOWAS comprise:

i.   Food and Agriculture;
ii. Industry, Science and Technology and Energy;
iii. Environment and Natural Resources;
iv. Transport, Communications and Tourism;
v.   Trade, Customs, Taxation, Statistics, Money and Payments;
vi. Political, Judicial and Legal Affairs, Regional Security and Immigration;
vii. Human Resources, Information, Social and Cultural Affairs;
viii. Administration and Finance Commission.

According to the Revised Treaty, the Authority of Heads of State and Government might restructure the Specialised Technical

Commissions or establish new ones, whenever it deems it necessary. (article 22) The Commissions are composed of representatives of Member States, and each establish subsidiary commissions to support it in carrying out its task. Under the advice of the Council of Ministers, the Commissions meet as frequently as required; they prepare their rules of procedure for the Council's approval. The functions of the Specialised Technical Commissions are to prepare projects and programmes within their fields of competence for the consideration of the Council of Ministers through the President of the Commission. The projects and programmes may be drawn on the initiative of the Commissions or at the request of either the Council or the ECOWAS Commission. The Commissions also ensure the coordination and harmonisation of projects and programmes, facilitate and monitor the application of the provisions of the Treaty and protocols pertaining to their domains of responsibility, and carry out other functions allocated to them. (article 23, 24)

After the July 2013 institutional reform, the ECOWAS now has six new departments, namely Human Resources Management; Education, Science and Culture; Energy and Mines; Telecommunications and Information Technology; Industry and Private Sector Promotion; and Finance and Administration.

Manifestly, the Treaty of ECOWAS has revealed a huge aspiration for integration and development in the economic sector, which is the principal reason for its existence. Its Revised Treaty, 1993, that, as we have seen, extended political and economic co-operation among Member States, and sets the achievement of a common market and a single currency as economic objectives. The same Treaty provides, in the political sphere, for a West African Parliament, an Economic and Social Council and an ECOWAS Court of Justice to replace the existing Tribunal and enforce Community decisions. The Treaty also formally assigned the Community the responsibility for preventing and settling regional conflicts.

The ambitions of the founders vis-à-vis the objectives of the ECOWAS defined by its Treaties have however not yet thoroughly been attained especially in its main domain, the economy, after nearly forty years of existence. The Organisation is progressively putting in place the modalities of free movement of citizens, goods and services in the community as stipulated in the 1979 Protocol A/P.1/5/79 relating to the free movement of people, residence and establishment, programmed to be implemented in stages within fifteen (15) years, but the project of a common currency[137] in West Africa, to replace the franc CFA,[138] and other currencies in the region, which was initiated during the 22nd Summit of Heads of State and Government, held in Lome, in December 1999, has been staggering.

It is worth highlighting that this project of monetary union, actually started as early as 1975, when the West Africa Clearing House (WACH)[139] was created. The objectives of the WACH were to promote the use of the currencies of member countries of the Clearing House in trade, and to motivate them to liberalise trade and promote economic and monetary arrangement amongst themselves. The WACH was therefore established as a means of payment for transactions among institutions within the Community. The West Africa Bankers' Association (WABA) as a professional association of financial and banking institutions and services, was subsequently established in 1978, to support the operations of the WACH, a scheme to which other financial and credit institutions joined. The Heads of State and Government of the Member States of the ECOWAS launched the ECOWAS Monetary Cooperation Programme (EMCP) nine years later, subsequently leading to the establishment of the West African Monetary Agency (WAMA) in

---

[137]The idea to have all the Member States of the ECOWAS use a single currency is as old as the Community itself when the West Africa Clearing House (WACH) was established as a mechanism for the payment of transactions between and among institutions within the member states..

[138] The CFA franc or *franc CFA* in French, is a currency used in twelve former French African colonies, as well as in Guinea-Bissau, a former Portuguese colony and in Equatorial Guinea, a former Spanish colony. The CFA franc is fixed to the euro at the rate of 100 CFA francs to 1 French (nouveau) franc, which equals to 0.152449 euro; (655.957 CFA francs = 1 euro). Until 1958, CFA meant *Colonies françaises d'Afrique* ("French colonies of Africa"). From this date (the French Fifth Republic), it stood for *Communauté française d'Afrique* ("French community of Africa"). Since Independence in the 1960s, CFA is taken to mean *Communauté Financière Africaine* (African Financial Community).

[139]WACH comprise the eight Central Banks of ECOWAS member States, including the Central Bank of West African States - *Banque Centrale des États de l'Afrique de l'Ouest*, (BCEAO), which is a central bank of the West African Economic and Monetary Union – Union Economique et Monétaire Ouest Africaine (UEMOA), i.e., seven francophone countries: Benin, Burkina Faso, Cote d'Ivoire, Mali, Niger, Senegal and Togo, and one lusophone country: Guinea Bissau.

1995, to ensure that the process was systematically linked to the ultimate creation of a single monetary zone in the Community. Collectively, the EMCP and WAMA aimed at adopting common policies to achieve a harmonised system and a common central institution in the region by the year 2000.

The main objective of this in the short term was to reinforce the methods of payment, which further led to the introduction of the ECOWAS Travellers' Cheque. In the medium term, the aim was to achieve limited currency convertibility, and in the long term, to achieve a single monetary zone in the sub-region characterised by the use of a common single currency and the creation of a common central bank.

The effective realisation of a common single currency is very vital for the sub-region in the sense that it will reduce the cost of transactions by avoiding the use of currencies foreign to the Community, for example the Dollar or the Euro. This helps to combat speculation and ensure price stability, which under normal circumstances stimulates trade and the growth of business within the Community. In the perspective of economic integration, the common currency will therefore render trade more effective in the West African region where a lot of informal trade takes place, which constitutes a huge loss in revenue, simply because informal traders do not pay tax on their transactions and the money conversions are usually carried out by illegal money dealers in unfair competition with banks and exchange bureaux. The single currency will also have the positive effect of disciplining countries in the economic partnership by coercing them to manage their economies more effectively to respect the criteria, which will further promote economic growth and development enabling the region to be competitive in international trade.

However, the monetary sector of the ECOWAS has been differentiated by two sub-groups: one consists of the eight UEMOA[140] countries, basically Francophone with a unique currency, the franc CFA as well as a customs union. The second group consists of the remaining seven ECOWAS Member States, mostly Anglophone, each of which has its own currency, namely the Cedi of Ghana, the Dalasi of The Gambia, the Escudo of Cape Verde, the Franc of Guinea (Conakry), the Dollar of Liberia, the Naira of Nigeria and the Leone

---

[140]*Union Economique et Monétaire Ouest Africaine.* The eight countries are Benin, Burkina Faso, Ivory Coast, Guinea Bissau, Mali, Niger, Senegal and Togo.

of Sierra Leone. Five[141] of the seven Member States have joined efforts in an institutional cooperative framework to establish a second monetary zone: the West African Monetary Zone (WAMZ), whose objective is to establish a common market characterised by a single currency and common central bank to replace the existing national currencies. The realisation of the common currency of ECOWAS has therefore necessitated the adoption, beforehand, of a common monetary and exchange rate policy of the West African Monetary Zone, i.e. countries out of the CFA zone, before a fusion of the two zones to institute the West African Common currency. In the framework of monetary cooperation of the ECOWAS, the WAMZ established the West African Monetary Institute (WAMI) in the Ghanaian capital, Accra, in March 2001, as an intermediary organ responsible for setting up the West African Central Bank (WACB).

For the WAMI to effectively monitor the creation of the proposed West African currency, member states of the WAMZ were expected to meet a set of primary and secondary macroeconomic convergence criteria before the monetary integration. The WAMI outlined the commitments of member countries to adopt policies that would allow price stability, including maintaining inflation rates inferior or equal to 5% of GDP as well as a sustainable fiscal position. Member countries of the West African Monetary Zone must build a stable situation of public finance and limit the financing of budget deficits to less than 10% tax revenue. Members of the zone also need to maintain efficient external reserves of about 6 months import cover, tax receipts of about 20% of GDP and the capacity to generate as much as about 20% of public investment from the domestic economy.

The anticipated common currency of the second zone has been named the ECO, and the initial date set for its introduction was January 2003. However by November 2002, it became cleared that the countries of the potential ECO zone would not manage to meet the convergence criteria, which consequently forced the ECOWAS to push the dates of introducing the ECO to July 2005, then to 2009, then to 2010 and then to 2015. The fusion of the franc CFA of the UEMOA and ECO of the WAMZ is now projected for 2020.

---

[141] The Gambia, Ghana, Guinea, Nigeria and Sierra Leone. Liberia and Cape Verde are not yet members but attend WAMZ meetings as observers.

The will to adopt a common currency in West Africa that in turn will undergo a probationary period of at least three years before it gets into the Community as a common currency for the fifteen (15) Member States has emerged from good intentions. However, the common single currency programme has not yet been successful, because of various factors. First of all the delay fixed to harmonise monetary policies has been apparently too short, consequently, the fifteen (15) countries involved in the project have found it enormously difficult to meet the convergence criteria, because the economies of the countries involved are at different stages of development. Also the ECOWAS intends to bring together the economies of two categories of countries essentially different: countries of the franc CFA zone that has an internationally convertible currency, and the others deprived of this advantage but some of whose demographic and economic weight are considerable, such as Nigeria. In the ECOWAS zone where there are several national currencies including the franc CFA, as we have seen, the differences amongst the currencies remain significant. For the economic integration and collective autonomy through a common market articulated around an economic and monetary union to be efficiently realisable, other measures must however be taken to avoid a situation in which some Member States impose their will on others with relatively weak economies. In short the economic adjustment programme of Member States of the ECOWAS must be structurally and efficiently planned. Also a credible monetary union necessitates the establishment of an effective and sustainable Customs union, which is yet to be effective in the Community.

The Community has suffered a huge diversity of resource and capacity limitation, because the Member States are different in their sizes, their natural resources, their states of development, their relations with the world market and their colonial histories. The Gambia with relatively few natural resources, and Liberia that has emerged from a ten-year civil war, have neither the same interests, nor the same economic potentials as huge petroleum producer Nigeria. Anglophone Ghana does not have the same economic objectives as Francophone Senegal. The convergence of economic and financial policies has therefore become a difficult mission considering these enormous disparities of interest and capabilities that exist amongst the Member States. Around the end of 2002, it became practically impossible to respect the calendar for monetary union scheduled for January 2003. The situation of economic convergence of Member States in the course of 2003 was judged insufficient. Therefore the principal shortcoming to the project of a common currency is the Member States' diversity of interests combined with their weakness in micro-economic convergence, illustrated by their inability to maintain fixed criteria. During meetings of the WAMZ in Conakry, Guinea, between August 30 and September 3, 2004, the Heads of State and Government asked the West African Monetary Institute to conduct a study to determine the positions of Member States with regards to the institution of the monetary union. The result of this study was exposed to the authorities during the meetings held in Banjul, The Gambia, between May 2 and 6, 2005 (wami-imao.ors).[142]

The Community is without doubt a bright architecture and a progressive form and attempt of regional economic integration, but these weaknesses that weigh on it hamper the capacity of its members to abide by the rules and follow a consistent strategy for a single currency.

The Protocol relating to the free movement of persons, residence and establishment adopted in Dakar in May 1979, followed by supplementary protocols, in 1986 and 1990 on the same issue, to be implemented in stages in fifteen (15) years, has, as indicated, been relatively progressive; however it has been put into difficulty by some Member States. The ECOWAS free trade area, which is known as the ECOWAS Trade Liberalisation Scheme (ETLS), aims at the free movement of transport, goods and persons within the Community, as well as the removal of all tariff and non-tariff barriers to trade, to promote greater economic growth. The long term objective of the Free Trade Area is to progress to a full customs union and ultimately

---

[142]The studies revealed that amongst other things, the situation of convergence has shown remarkable results in 2004 relative to 2003. Nigeria and The Gambia have met three most important criteria in 2004, two in 2003 and inflation has continued to slow down. Sierra Leone has recorded appreciable results going from respect for no criterion to one in 2003, to two important criteria in 2004, while Guinea has improved its performance from non-respect of the criteria in 2003 to one first rank criterion in 2004. Ghana maintained the two criteria that it respected in 2003. In brief the criteria of the West African Monetary Zone have not totally been met and in that condition no single country is eligible to the monetary union.

131

a common market to facilitate trade in the region. However the implementation of the ETLS has so far not been effectively successful. On the issue of free movement of persons, the Authority of Heads of State and Government adopted and launched the ECOWAS passport at its 23rd session in Abuja, in May 2000, in view of the ECOWAS citizenship. The ECOWAS passport was to progressively replace national passports within the period of five years. However, up to now, the majority of Member States have not yet issued the passport to their citizens. Also, although the Community has abolished visas there are still some difficulties in implementing the ECOWAS protocols guaranteeing migrant workers in other Member States their rights as citizens of the Community, and for entrepreneurs to rightfully settle in other Member States of the Community. There are still a large number of checkpoints which pose unvarying sources of harassment for ECOWAS travellers.

Nigeria, which massively expelled citizens of other Member States including Benin, Burkina Faso and Ghana in 1984, had argued that the protocol of free movement of people did not authorise living in the country beyond 90 days and that the stay should not be accompanied by a search for work. Nigeria is in fact underprivileged with regards to immigration, because its relative economic prosperity has attracted citizens of other Member States.

Apart from the difficulties concerning the free movement of people in the Community, the lifting of Customs and Excise duties has also met with some problems at the frontiers and Customs posts in many Member States of the community. Some acts of fraud have been reported on the highway that goes from Cotonou, Benin to Niamey, (Niger). The situation is similar between the ports of Lomé, (Togo) and Ouagadougou, (Burkina Faso). Member States have therefore taken measures to remedy the problem by creating national committees to follow-up the programmes on the free movement of people and goods, which has led to the establishment of an insurance card, today in service in many Member States.

Some countries in the Community might have reasonably feared that the reduction or the outright elimination of Customs and Excise duties with regional partners would deprive them of an important source of revenue. The sources of income from Customs and Excise being in general limited, fear of losing revenue coming from Customs duties could further hinder trade liberalisation in the Community, except if the compensation fund that has been put in place is effectively administered. The treaty of ECOWAS envisaged payment of compensation subject to losses in revenue in relation to Customs and Excise duties to relatively small and less competitive Member States unable to stand competition from other Member States.

The ECOWAS Travellers' Cheque, introduced in 1998, after several postponements, was supposed to be a practical, efficient and simple means of payment that should allow paying for expenses in any ECOWAS Member State or obtaining cash in the national currencies. Businessmen, tourists or ordinary travellers could pay for their hotel expenses, acquire merchandise and even procure local currencies in banks and exchange bureaux. They were therefore to facilitate payments, and accordingly satisfy users. However the ECOWAS Travellers' Cheques have been only slightly successful due primarily to inadequate publicity and bureaucratic bottlenecks. The West African Bankers Association (WABA), in Nigeria had advised that for ECOWAS Travellers' Cheques to be successful there was a need for massive public awareness in order to ensure adequate public knowledge and patronage for it. (modernghana.com) This instrument of payment was supposed to reduce the disparities amongst the values of the currencies in the Community. As a result it shows the will of Member States of the ECOWAS to reinforce the process of economic integration in the zone.

In terms of the maintenance of peace and security, the ECOWAS is recognised as having the most advanced peace and security arrangement amongst the economic communities in Africa. This is aided by its mandate to intervene not only politically, but also militarily in its Member States in case of the imminence of serious social disaster and a threat to peace and security, especially when an attempt has been made to overthrow democratically elected governments. The Community equally has the authority to intervene in situations where the human rights of its citizens have been threatened or violated. The ECOWAS' approach to deal with conflicts emerged from the principle that without peace, integration and development are not possible. Therefore in spite of enormous difficulties and setbacks, the peacekeeping mechanism of the ECOWAS has had relatively more success. The Community has also been more active in the procedure of mediation as a means of finding preventive measures and lasting peaceful solutions to conflicts in its Member States.

Through the ECOMOG, the ECOWAS has therefore played a primary role in extinguishing several conflicts in West Africa. It helped end the war in Liberia, subsequently facilitating democratic elections in July 1997. The ECOMOG also reversed the military coup in Sierra Leone, and reinstated democratic rule in that country in 1998, which ultimately gave way to the United Nations Mission in Sierra Leone (UNAMSIL) after the 1998 Lome agreement. The ECOWAS has made successful interventions in Guinea Bissau to reverse different military overthrows, the most recent being the April 2012 coup d'état just about two weeks before the second round of the presidential election. The coup-makers were forced to return power to civilians, which led to the organisation of successful democratic elections in April and May 2014. The ECOMOG also contributed enormously to the ceasefire and maintenance of peace between the government and "rebels" in the Ivorian civil conflict in 2002. The three ECOWAS summits held in the Ghanaian capital, Accra, after the eruption of the conflict in Ivory Coast, and the intervention of 3,000 ECOMOG soldiers, did not initially bring a concrete solution to the conflict, largely because of the intransigence of the two sides in the conflict. In the long run the ECOWAS succeeded in bringing the two enemy parties to the table and has effectively maintained peace in this country, at least before the post-electoral crisis, in the resolution of which again it played an important role. Just recently, in collaboration with the African Union and the United Nations Organisation, the ECOWAS put an end to the conflict caused by the invasion of northern Mali by Islamists, which followed the March 2012 coup d'état. Working with other continental and international organisations such as the African Union, the United Nations Organisation, the Commonwealth and the Francophonie, the ECOWAS has effectively contained most of the political problems that have emerged in its Member States.

In the domain of culture and languages the ECOWAS has manifested enormous interest and capacity, aware of the fact that economic integration and development in a community cannot be effective without the cultures and languages of the people of the community in question. This is why in Article 62 (c) of its Treaty, the ECOWAS manifested the desire to adopt an African language as a working language, in partnership with the existing official languages inherited from colonisation, namely English, French and Portuguese. At the sixth meeting of the ad hoc Committee in Charge of

Monitoring and Evaluating the Implementation of the ECOWAS Culture Development and Integration Programme, organised in Cotonou, Benin from April 16 to 19, 2012, the African Academy of Languages (ACALAN) as a specialised institution of the African Union mandated to empower African languages, was invited to propose a way forward on the choice of a common working West African Language for ECOWAS. The ACALAN proposed three Vehicular Cross-border Languages in West Africa, namely Fulfulde, Hausa and Madenkan as working languages of the ECOWAS. At the same meeting, delegates prepared the Terms of Reference and modalities for the institution of Cultural Industries as a Creative Enterprise, and a West African Cultural Institute (WACI). This shows that the ECOWAS has strategically considered adopting the cultures and languages of the West African region as part of the building blocks of socio-economic integration and development in the Community.

The problems caused by the two main colonial cultures in Francophone and Anglophone West Africa, and their consequent rivalries, have adversely affected reconstruction efforts in the region. However when the Member States of the *Communauté Economique de l'Afrique de l'Ouest* (CEAO),[143] now *Union économique et monétaire ouest africain* (UEMOA),[144] and their compatriots in Anglophone West Africa joined hands to create the ECOWAS, the recommended solution became the intensification of cooperation between the two zones that do not differ in their need for reconstruction. The only difference was their colonial histories and the official languages they use in administration; but the ECOWAS became regionally more open, because it is relatively larger and relatively more independent. The existence of the two monetary zones does not seem to pose any problem, since the Member States of the Community are consciously aspiring to a common independent currency.

The ECOWAS is considered by far the most effective Economic Community in Africa in almost all domains, but the overall result obtained by the Community after nearly forty years of existence, as we have noted, has not matched its ambitions, for several complex reasons, some of which have already been mentioned. The mediocrity

---

[143]Economic Community of West Africa
[144]West African Economic and Monetary Union.

of the markets in the Community offers poor economic prospect to West African States. This has adversely affected ECOWAS projects, especially in the presence of big international commercial blocs. The multiplicity of institutions and associations having very similar, or sometimes the same objectives and the concomitant membership of the majority of Member States of the Community of several associations, have inevitably provoked conflicts of interest and inefficiency.[145] To these weaknesses, the problem of funding has been added. Some Member States of the ECOWAS have difficulty in paying their contributions. A huge problem has, in the past decades, also been created by the lack of political will, appropriate democracy and human rights by some individual Member States. These have caused enormous problems by instigating conflicts and political instability, consequently impinging on economic activities and development. There is a lack of formality of commercial activities, and little cooperation between West African central banks. The application of certain protocols of the Treaty of ECOWAS becomes sensitive and delicate because they directly affect the national interests of some Member States. Nigeria, for example, is the most vulnerable to the protocol of free movement of citizens and goods, provoking massive immigration to the country, because of its relative economic prosperity.

Nonetheless, there is a great desire by West Africans to promote economic progress, integration and peace, and the spirit of solidarity that determines the emerging forces behind the continuity is progressively growing in strength. All these difficulties encountered by the ECOWAS do not therefore prevent it from undertaking the project of a common single currency, which is going on. The inception of the European Common Market took thirty-five years to become a reality and the establishment of a common European currency took even longer.[146] This should serve Africans as a lesson of courage that nothing has been lost. ECOWAS has only thirty-nine

---

[145] This multiplicity of institutions and associations having similar or even the same objectives and the concomitant membership of several associations is not exclusive to ECOWAS, it equally affects the African Union and almost all global international organisations.

[146] It took Western Europe 44 years to realise a common currency, from the establishment of the European Economic Community (EEC) or the European Community in 1957 to the introduction of the Euro on 1st January 2002 by twelve European Union Member States.

years of existence, but that lesson of courage should not be taken for granted.

The reforms of the revised Treaty of ECOWAS, signed by the Heads of State during the 16th summit of the ECOWAS in Cotonou in July 1993, awakened high hopes in the Community. These reforms envisage the creation of new institutional apparatuses such as the Economic and Social Council to represent the civil society, and a Community Court of Justice to replace the community Tribunal. The new Treaty has also created a Community Parliament, a mechanism of direct regional taxation, and a Code for community investment. No country, apart from Mauritania,[147] has ever questioned its membership of the ECOWAS. The fact that it continues to exist is already an achievement for the West African people, because that shows their determination to face the many hurdles standing in front of their reconstruction efforts, including the artificial colonial barriers of languages.

Policy-makers are thus continuing their efforts, in spite of all these problems, to make the process of economic integration more evocative. For example, the ECOWAS Commission has drawn up a Regional Poverty Reduction Strategy that supports national strategies and proposes a joint strategic framework to provide external aid to Member States as a means of accelerating regional integration. Owing to the adoption of the Protocol on Democracy and Good Governance that aims at strengthening intra-communal peace, democracy and stability, relative peace and stability have gradually established the process of democracy in the West African region. This protocol provides the ECOWAS election monitoring and observation process that has contributed enormously to the organisation of relatively free and fair elections and to the promotion of democratic institutions in Member States. Apart from the politico-military agitations in Mali and the two Guineas,[148] the governments of

---

[147] Mauritania decided to quit ECOWAS in 2002, because of "the organisation's decision to establish a common currency by 2004," and Mauritania is not ready to give up its own currency, the Ouguiya. However, the real reason for Mauritania's departure from ECOWAS was said to be based more on the fact that it did not have the desire to integrate in Sub-Saharan Africa or participate in the Common Market. The proof is that Mauritania has not paid its membership contribution to ECOWAS for the last 16 years, since Colonel Ould Taya seized power through a coup d'état in 1984.

all the Member States of the ECOWAS have been democratically elected in the formal sense of democracy. The recent coups d'état in the Community have been brilliantly dealt with by the ECOWAS, by communally leaning on the Protocol on Democracy and Good Governance and imposing financial, economic and diplomatic sanctions on the perpetrators of the coups d'état in Mali and Guinea Bissau. The coup leaders of both Mali and Guinea Bissau had to agree to conditions imposed by the ECOWAS for transition to democracy. Therefore, in Mali and Guinea Bissau, democratic elections were conducted in late 2013 and early 2014 respectively. This is remarkable progress, because in spite of the non-aggression pact of 1978 and the 1981 protocol on mutual defence, the West African region was affected by intermittent instability in the form of civil and military conflicts, caused by the lack of democratic rule and the principles of human rights. The West African region has now enjoyed relative peace and security, thanks to the efforts of the ECOWAS.

The transformation of the ECOWAS Secretariat into the ECOWAS Commission is a key reform that aims at increased democratisation of the policies and administration of the Community. The citizens of the Member States are also now becoming progressively more involved in the affairs of the Community and those of their countries through representation in the new ECOWAS parliament, whose members, we have seen, are chosen from national parliaments. In the domain of international relations, ECOWAS is consequently enjoying more recognition now. Firstly it had been mandated by the African Union to implement and coordinate the NEPAD and other programmes in West Africa. For example, the ECOWAS has been entrusted with the mandate to harmonise and coordinate the implementation of the framework of the

---

[148] On March 2, 2009 the president of Guinea Bissau João Bernardo Vieira, was assassinated by the army in what was alleged to have been a revenge attack following the killing of the country's military chief. On December 23, 2008, shortly after the death of President Lansana Conté, in Guinea Conakry, a section of the army lead by Captain Moussa Dadis Camara called the National Council for Democracy and Development (CNDD) declared a coup d'état. Mutinying Malian soldiers, displeased with the management of the Tuareg rebellion in North Mali, attacked the presidential palace, state television, and military barracks on 21 March, 2012. The soldiers,who had formed the National Committee for the Restoration of Democracy and State ended up overthrowing the government of Amadou Toumani Touré forcing him into hiding..

Comprehensive African Agricultural Development Programme (CAADP)[149] in the West African sub-region with national authorities. Secondly, it is a key partner of the United Nations Organisation especially in the domains of economic development and the maintenance of peace and security in the West African region. The current ECOWAS Vision 2020 project, which is a long-term strategic plan seeking to provide a reference point for an integrated development approach for the West Africa region, in line with a bottom up strategy of involving community citizens for a people-centred Community development approach, is a demonstration of more commitments by the West African people to closer integration. For example through the West African Civil Society Forum (WACSOF) and other similar civil society groups, the ECOWAS Commission is promoting the active involvement of ordinary citizens in the affairs of their Community. The ECOWAS Agricultural Policy (ECOWAP), whose objective is to guarantee food security and sovereignty as a means of reducing dependence on imports by giving priority to food production and processing is another bright example of the efforts of the Community to promote economic growth and development, in all the sectors of the Community. The ECOWAP was adopted in January 2005 by the Authority of Heads of State and Government of ECOWAS, on the notion that national (agricultural) policies should be aligned with the global regional policy.

Considering these positive elements, despite the main problem of resource and capacity limitation, the ECOWAS is really at a crossroads of African reconstruction. The community is, in this new millennium, enjoying relative peace and stability after decades of civil and politico-military wars. The region had been destabilised by the violence of the late 1980s and the 1990s, including massive refugee displacements due to wars, which disrupted economic activities and caused widespread diseases.

One of the objectives of the ECOWAS Commission should henceforth be the continuous effective running of the compensation

---

[149] The Comprehensive African Agricultural Development Program (CAADP) is initiated by African Governments under the auspices of the African Union/New Partnership for African Development (AU/NEPAD) to accelerate economic growth and development of African countries. It is an agriculture led development scheme seeking to eliminate hunger, increase food and nutrition security, improve well-being, and facilitate the expansion of exports.

scheme in their common tariff project. European and North American experiences should serve as lessons for Africans, since integration requires the effective implementation of protocols, declarations and measures to reduce inequalities. Even if these inequalities are not necessarily produced by the process of the integration in question, the reduction of such disparities depends on the good functioning of the process. If we consider the case of the European Union, it disposes of a number of mechanisms that allow Member States to assist others in a relatively weaker economic situation. The ECOWAS Member States should equally find the means of effectively remedying such inequalities in the zone. The bigger and economically stronger Member States of the community should therefore strengthen the moral responsibility of sacrifice and solidarity that the Community has been exercising. As with the European Economic Community, the ECOWAS Commission must show that the vital characteristics of the harmonisation of general economic policies imply that each government disposes of some power and capacity of control over the dominant forces of the national economy. This power must not be reduced by lack of efficacy, and the fear of losing sovereignty; it must instead be strengthened by the need for integration and reconstruction.

Conclusion

The institutions of slavery, Colonialism and apartheid have transformed African socio-economic institutions to the point of annihilating them, and as such confiscated the peoples' power and sovereignty to administer their own affairs and determine their own destiny. Consequently the existence of these oppressive institutions triggered Nationalism as a form of resistance to regain African values and systems in an effort to repair the damages caused by them. African Nationalism has distinguished itself from other forms of Nationalism as is traditionally known in most Western States, in the sense that it was based more on resistance and the reacquisition of sovereignty than the glorification of African identities and/or the demonstration of national supremacy. It was a unique trend in the sense that it was the entire continent that had been invaded and humiliated; consequently the whole of Africa has participated in this collective responsibility. Nationalism in the form of resistance against Imperialism continued through to the post-independence era.

Between 1935 and 1980 there were very important contacts between Sub-Saharan Africa and the West, particularly North America. Firstly these contacts were marked by the presence of African students in mostly American universities. Secondly the migration that was promoted by the Back to Africa Movement[150] in the United States encouraged African-American missionaries to go to Africa in order to evangelise Sub-Saharan Africans. This two-way movement formally contributed enormously to West African Nationalism. African students in American universities participated in conferences and other socio-academic activities, enabling them to exchange ideas with their American counterparts.

Nationalism in West Africa was inspired by Pan-Negroism in the Americas that, in the beginning, centred on a psychological and cultural quest for the identity and self-respect of black people, especially the Black African Diaspora. The principal objective of Pan-Negroism was, first of all, to fight against discrimination and racism

---

[150]The African Colonization movement, also known as the Back-to-Africa movement, originated in the United States in the 19th century. It encouraged people of African descent to return to Africa, homeland of their ancestors. The movement would eventually inspire other movements ranging from the Nation of Islam to the Rastafarian movement.

of which black people, especially in the Diaspora, had been victims. When Pan-Negroism was imported to West Africa by Kwame Nkrumah and his comrades after World War II, they transformed it to Pan-Africanism, with a purely revolutionary face focusing on a struggle with an entirely political purpose to liberate Africa from the shackles of European colonisation and Imperialism. World War II and the Atlantic Charter had also been factors of enlightenment for Sub-Saharan Africa in its struggle for independence, because through them Africans claimed the right to choose the form of government under which they would live, and wished to have the sovereign rights and self-government of which they had been forcibly deprived restored.

From Kwame Nkrumah's return to Ghana in 1947 to the establishment of the Organisation of African Unity in 1963, he advanced his theories and ideologies designating the methods that the African continent should apply to achieve territorial unity, and to assure socio-economic security and development. It was this innovative aspect principally endorsed by Nkrumah that contributed to the Independence of Ghana, and progressively to liberating the rest of Sub-Saharan Africa from Colonialism. The Independence of Ghana in West Africa was thus the pillar of Sub-Saharan African Independence and Kwame Nkrumah was the main draughtsman. Since this date Africans have continued to fight for their liberty and their human dignity through the inception of the Organisation of African Unity (OAU). In spite of differences of ideologies between the "revolutionaries" and the "moderates," African leaders of the immediate post-colonial era fought for the liberation of the rest of Africa and for integration.

The first phase of immediate post-colonial Nationalism was, however, not entirely successful because Independence only liberated Sub-Saharan Africa politically, and even that not wholly. Kwame Nkrumah's aspirations for a united Africa to effectively wipe out all forces of Imperialism and to promote sustainable socio-economic development did not materialise. Immediate post-colonial Nationalism was not totally revolutionary because it centred more on the political aspect of the struggle, exclusively focusing on breaking the chains of Colonialism in Africa, and almost ignoring important domains such as the economy and culture. The fact that Africans almost neglected the post-colonial imperial angle concerning the economic and cultural domains posed enormous problems, because no liberation struggle is complete without economic and cultural self-determination. The Pan-African struggle should have also considered the economic and social aspects of African reconstruction by advancing economic and socio-cultural Nationalism, political and economic democracy and human rights in an African context.

The first negative effect of Imperialism on African reconstruction was at the level of African unity, after the divergence of Africans into the Monrovia and Casablanca groups principally. The Cold War had engendered and aggravated this situation, for each of the two divergent groups in Africa followed one of the two antagonist ideologies of the two blocs which had engaged in ideological warfare. The notion of immediate political and economic union of the Casablanca group was opposed to the idea of progressive union of the pro-Western Monrovia group. The Casablanca group radically defended its programme of immediate unity for Africa to acquire "real Independence" and promote socio-economic development. But the fact that it affiliated its ideologies to the Soviet bloc was apparently another setback for African reconstruction, because it exposed the continent to another form of Imperialism however comparatively less binding that might be.

If the OAU succeeded, through its Liberation Committee in collaboration with other international organisations and associations, notably the United Nations Organisation, in liberating African countries still under colonial rule, and subsequently liberating South Africa from apartheid, its project of integration, continental peace and socio-economic development did not thoroughly succeed. Africa today is formally decolonised but practically still under imperial influence. We have indicated that the failure of the first phase of post-colonial Nationalism was due to several factors amongst which the colonial/imperial factor has been paramount and almost omnipresent. In this phase of the African Renaissance, the new African Union is exposed to the same dangers if this imperial obstacle and the economic and cultural dependence of Africa on the West remain in place.

The notion of territorial integrity in the Charter of the OAU had also been an obstacle to African reconstruction, since unity and the strict notion of sovereignty are incompatible.[151] Articles 3 and 4 on

---

[151] If we take the USA as an example, each of the 50 states has its sovereignty, but

non-interference caused a lot of confusion in the efforts of the OAU to effectively and lastingly resolve conflicts. Regionalism[152] is perhaps an inevitable aspect of most socio-economic relations at continental level, but we have seen that in the case of African Nationalism, it has been used excessively, almost destroying the efforts, and symbolising weakness and a lack of proper vision. Regionalism in the form of the unwillingness of individual African States to shed a portion of their national autonomy has stalled the process of African reconstruction. Since the creation of the OAU in 1963, most leaders have worked very hard to avoid losing even a fraction of the sovereignty of their States, and resisted all attempts to change the present geopolitical setup drawn by European colonisers in Berlin. Kwame Nkrumah struggled for a Federation of African States,[153] but these shortcomings made him lose the battle, because some of his compatriots were suspicious about his motivation. The spirit of unity is therefore often rejected by the defence of national sovereignty. In fact, individual States are more apprehensive about losing their sovereignty than they are conscious about the benefits of integration. Integration requires a strong will to transfer sovereignty to the benefit of community institutions.

Religious rivalry notably between the two principal faiths, Christianity and Islam, introduced or developed during the slave trade and Colonialism has also had an impact on African Nationalism and reconstruction. Spiritual antagonism has created division in Africa, in individual States, having the effect of creating and amplifying conflict.

After independence African countries were unconsciously blasé in the Pan-African ideal, and stampeded towards drawing and signing protocols and treaties on regional and continental integration, but

---

the Federal Government of the United States is the central United States governmental body, established by the United States Constitution. The Federal Government has overriding powers in most domains of government. The term Big Government, which is mostly used by conservatives and laissez-faire advocates to describe a government that is excessively large and inappropriately involved in certain areas of public and private sectors, has been readily accepted in American politics since the election of Ronald Reagan.

[152]The term regionalism is principally applied to mean devotion to the interests of one's own country or region.

[153]We have used the term Federation of African States to avoid copying the term of United States of Africa, which might cause confusion with the already existing United States of America.

very few of these were effectively executed. There was very little conviction and resolve, symbolised by the enormous detachment between the declarations during regular reunions and their corresponding actions. The project of African unity was also almost monopolised by political governments neglecting the mass. Therefore the civil society felt less involved, even to the point of being disinterested, which puts a burden on the engagement of the OAU.

Pragmatic African approaches to regional integration such as the Lagos Plan of Action (1980),[154] tried to accord a preponderant role to the States. However a good number of African governments have not got the natural and/or financial resources that can enable them to execute corresponding policies.

Africa's problems were also aggravated by corruption[155] at many levels. These factors as well as the divisions spawned by the Cold War adversely affected the emergence of effective governments on the continent. Most African countries were also almost terminally paralysed by civil and military conflicts that killed economic activities and progress.

Colonialism has created an almost irreparable dissimilarity amongst the African countries. The relationship between the principal divisions, Anglophone Africa and Francophone Africa has been a fundamental obstacle. Newly independent countries maintained close economic and cultural ties with their former colonisers. The Gambia, Ghana, Nigeria and Sierra Leone with Great

---

[154]The Lagos Plan of Action drafted in Lagos, Nigeria in April 1980, during a conference of African leaders, is officially known as the Lagos Plan of Action for the Economic Development of Africa, 1980–2000. It was an OAU-backed plan to increase the self-sufficiency of the African continent, and was characterised as the continent's response to the World Bank's 1981 Berg Report, titled "Accelerated Development in Sub-Saharan Africa.' The plan blamed the Structural Adjustment Programme, the IMF and the World Bank for Africa's economic crisis. It also blamed the vulnerability of African economies on worldwide economic shocks, such as the oil crisis of 1973.

[155]Corruption is not an exclusive African problem; it is an international problem. It is also present in Western governments, like France and the United Kingdom. For example the recent MPs expenses scandal in the UK. However corruption has an adverse effect on African reconstruction simply because resources that were meant for specific projects were sometimes destructively diverted for personal use, just like in most countries in the world.

Britain, and the Francophone countries, Senegal, Mali, Ivory Coast with France, even though this phenomenon has been more pronounced with the Francophone countries. The concomitant existence of the *Communauté Economique d'Afrique de l'Ouest* (CEDAO), now *Union Economique et Monétaire Ouest Africaine* (UEMOA) and the Economic Community of West African States (ECOWAS) illustrated these shortcomings. All these deficiencies have shown that Africa is only nominally independent.

The diverse levels of development in Africa and the extreme poverty of some countries caused partly by slavery and colonial exploitation have had an adverse effect on African reconstruction. Most African countries principally produce a few cash crops destined for export. This condition generated by the colonial system of production created a situation in which some African countries have very little to exchange amongst themselves in the perspective of commerce. Therefore some huge and rich countries might not see any real economic advantage in integrating with relatively small and poor countries if it is not to exercise some political influence on them for prestige, or for the sake of a mere ideology of African Continentalism.

The result of all this is that after more than 60 years of independence, Africa subsists almost in socio-economic poverty and marginalisation. Frantz Fanon symbolised Africa as "The Wretched of the Earth" in the context of globalisation today, in one of his works which bears that title. As long as the continent does not wake up and live in the political and socio-cultural domains, economic development and the entire project of reconstruction will remain perpetually stagnant. In this context, the project of African integration should be a common front to affront a capitalist world especially the imperialist West aggressively trying to marginalise the continent. This is the reason why African leaders have developed new modalities of integration, such as the transformation of the Organisation of African Unity to the African Union. The new African Union thus represents a continuity of efforts and symbolises the perpetual desire of the African leaders and people for effective reconstruction.

Therefore the transformation of the Organisation of African Unity to the African Union symbolised some failure to maintain the force that African Nationalism had exercised on Imperialism. The OAU's error from the beginning was that it exclusively concentrated on political struggle for a long time, giving precedence to sovereignty, and paying little attention to other spheres, notably the economy and culture. Also a lot of alliances or associations in Africa have been based on uncoordinated initiatives.

But Africa seems to know by now that economic development does not automatically follow political independence, and that no process of development is effective and sustainable without the culture and languages of the people concerned.

The proliferation of institutions for integration in Africa is a manifest sign of weakness, hesitation, and the dispersal of ideologies and capabilities to embark on constructive projects. The problem is accentuated by multiple factors, including erroneous choices and poor economic priorities and planning, duplication of projects and the absence of rigour in management and administration. All these weaknesses have been aggravated by the world economic crises, especially the recent sub-prime crisis that started in the USA.

The two principal components of post-colonial Nationalism in West Africa were Pan-Africanism and Negritude, and the two principal actors were Kwame Nkrumah and Léopold Sédar Senghor respectively; however each carried out his struggle with a different strategy. Negritude as a neologism was a literary and cultural movement of black Francophone intellectuals in Paris, even if it later contained a slight notion of anti-colonial rhetoric. It was a formulation of African diasporic identity, overwhelmingly asserting pride in black culture and heritage. It laid emphasis on Marcus Garvey's words that black people are "descendants of the greatest and proudest race who ever peopled the earth." (africaspeaks.com). Its original conception attributed to Césaire was a developmental model based on resistance that perceives the particularity of the black man as a historical phenomenon. Through its literature, it affirmed the personality of black people, redefining their collective experience of domination borne by slavery and Colonialism, and all their moral and psychological implications. It awakened the cultural awareness of the black man to the dangers of Western ideology that perpetually humiliated him. Negritude, however, as presented by Léopold Sédar Senghor did not play a determining role in the political struggle for the liberation, reconstruction and economic development of Sub-Saharan Africa in a general context.

147

Senghor gradually modified Césaire's formulation in his writings and debates, giving it an essentialist interpretation, arguing that the essence of the existence of black people was unchanged. Senghor's concept was broadly criticised, being accused of using the term ideologically for a political purpose, when he was President of Senegal. His version of Negritude nonetheless continued to present a model for the ongoing struggle of black liberation at least spiritually.

Contrary to Kwame Nkrumah and the other actors of African Nationalism, the principal African proponent of Negritude, Léopold Sédar Senghor, did not want to entertain any form of opposition between the West and Africa. Negritude in fact distinguished itself from Pan-Africanism in that it was only its original founder from Martinique, Aimé Césaire, as we have seen, who adopted a relatively more revolutionary or radical view of the movement. His African counterpart, Léopold Sédar Senghor, who adopted the term, attached as we have seen an essentially literary and cultural notion to it, showing off the value and the pride of African cultures as a reaction to their sufferings. He based it on complementarities instead of antagonism of black and white cultures, of the black and white races, attaching a notion of assimilation to it. Senghor believed that Colonialism certainly tampered with, and even disrupted African pre-colonial socio-economic and political structures, but that African independence signified that Colonialism belonged to the past. In that context there is no more antipathy between the former colonisers and Africa. Senghorian Negritude can therefore only loosely be attached to African Nationalism in the socio-political sense of the word, because its contribution was based on the mere enrichment of the black man's culture, as Nkrumah put it, which could only partially be linked with Sub-Saharan Africa's reconstruction. Pan-Africanism agitated the world socio-politically whilst Negritude constructed its ideologies on a cultural notion without strictly engaging political and economic battles for African liberation and reconstruction. The reason for this, we have seen, was due to the different modes of administration of the two former colonial masters, the United Kingdom and France, as well as to the upbringing of Senghor.

Paradoxically it was the African Nationalists themselves who initiated the transformation of the two institutions into multicultural associations with the former colonial masters. The Commonwealth of Nations between Britain and its former dominions and colonies, and the Francophonie between France and its former colonies, are institutions borne from Colonialism.[156]

The Commonwealth of Nations and the Francophonie have undeniably been useful to African Member States in the sense that, since their inception, they have been catalysts of solidarity and development to a certain degree. The Commonwealth has been useful to Sub-Saharan Africa especially in the fight against apartheid, and in the struggle for the independence of some countries in Southern Africa that were massively inhabited by European settlers, notably Southern Rhodesia (Zimbabwe), even if that was achieved in an atmosphere of controversy.[157] Through the Commonwealth Fund for Technical Cooperation(CFTC) established in 1971, the Technical Assistant Group(TAG), and the Export Market Development (EMD), the Commonwealth has greatly helped its members in the domain of socio-economic and technological development. The Commonwealth Fund for Technical Co-operation(CFTC) has in particular been supportive of the efforts of Member States in the field of investment, financial and debt management, public sector development, education and health. The Commonwealth has created a mutual and voluntary fund to which members contribute in accordance with their ability, but they draw on it according to their needs. It also provides technical expertise to both the public and private sectors through assignments that can last up to three years. Thanks to the lobbying of the former British Prime Minister, Tony Blair and his Chancellor of the Exchequer, Gordon Brown[158] (later

---

[156] The creation of the Commonwealth Secretariat was proposed in 1964 by a group of former English colonies including Ghana and Nigeria. The Francophonie, created in 1968, was also initiated by President Léopold Sédar Senghor of Senegal, and his compatriots, to continue cultural and linguistic ties with the former colonial master.

[157] Independence in this context refers to that of the accession of the black Africans to power. The Unilateral Declaration of Independence of Rhodesia from the United Kingdom was signed on November 11, 1965 by the administration of Ian Smith, whose Rhodesia Front Party opposed black majority rule in the then British colony. It declared Independence from the United Kingdom, but maintained allegiance to the Queen. The British government and many organisations including the Commonwealth and the United Nations condemned the move. The country gained what many called "real independence" of Zimbabwe with Robert Mugabe as Prime Minister in 1980. It is the period from 1980 that we refer to as Zimbabwean Independence.

Prime Minister), and the Ministers of Finance of Member States of the Commonwealth of Nations, the debt of developing countries, especially some Sub-Saharan African countries, was partially cancelled.

It is however important to underline that membership of these associative institutions, especially the fact that the proposition for their transformation partly came from the former colonial subjects, especially in Africa, seems to show that either Africa could not or was not ready to completely break the link with their former colonial masters. Most Africans have expressed the view that African members have been dominated by their former colonial masters in these associations. Even if the African Member States are independent to a certain degree, especially on problems affecting African countries in the Commonwealth of Nations, the United Kingdom seems to have relatively more influence in the running of the association, and the same observation is valid for France in the Francophonie. Therefore even if the principal prescribed goals of the two associations are, as stipulated in their Charters, to promote democracy and human rights, as well as sustainable socio-economic development in the Member States, they symbolise the incongruity of African Nationalism, especially in the perspectives of culture and languages.

The Commonwealth Development Corporation (CDC) through the Commonwealth Financial Assistance Plan (CFAP) financially helps members from developing countries, but the money used in these projects is mostly provided by the original members of the Commonwealth: Great Britain, Australia, Canada and New Zealand. Being an association that brings together the former coloniser and their former subjects, it is difficult for the Commonwealth to escape from the notion of imperial influence especially if the relationship involves financial assistance that mainly comes from the former to the latter. The argument goes that very few countries can voluntarily and genuinely shed their domination over others; therefore if the United Kingdom was forced by circumstances to formally liberate its former African colonies, it is not improbable that it tries other means to keep some influence over them, and the Commonwealth accordingly seems to be one of those means of re-exercising (indirect) influence.

---

[158] Gordon Brown served as the Prime Minister of the United Kingdom and Leader of the Labour Party from 2007 and 2010 after the resignation of Tony Blair.

The official language of the Commonwealth is English, and no other African language, even Kiswahili, is used as a working language. Its headquarters are at Marlborough House in the English capital, and the British Monarch has been symbolic Head of the Commonwealth since the former British colonies became members starting with India in 1949. The London Declaration allows Republics to retain membership, acknowledging the British Monarch as Head of the Commonwealth. In fact the Commonwealth is as monarchical as Britain herself, because it only changes Secretaries General like Britain changes Prime Ministers, but the position of Head of the Commonwealth (king or queen) is hereditary just like the Head of State of the United Kingdom, even if the leadership of the British monarch of the Commonwealth is said to be only symbolic. The Commonwealth of Nations could have created a rotational form of leadership, for example, the President of The Gambia, Ghana or Nigeria or other Member States as not only a symbolic head, but a real leader of the Commonwealth for a certain number of years, just as at the African Union. The Francophonie has no symbolic head; it only has a Secretary General carrying out its mandate under the authority of its three main institutions: the Summit, the Ministerial Conference and the Permanent Council.

Africa is apparently the only continent that imports almost everything, from basic necessities to university education and technologies, yet most of the raw materials which are the source of these items are from Africa. The judicial system in The Gambia, Nigeria, Ghana and Sierra Leone were copies of the English legal system based on Common Law, even if these countries have integrated traditional and/or religious elements into their legal systems. Most of the Francophone countries in West Africa have adopted French civil law, and almost all refer to Paris in the same way, and it is the same in most domains. This situation symbolises the continuity of colonial culture in Africa, which evokes Imperialism, a result of incomplete decolonisation that has created the condition of dependency. Therefore African civilisation and creativity have been adversely affected, meaning that African reconstruction has been haphazard so far. In fact African independence seemed to be voluntarily ill-defined and poorly devised right from the beginning, making reliance on support from the former colonial powers indispensable for the newly independent African countries, especially in the economic domain.

The year 1975 marked another important change in the nationalist struggle of West Africa. It was the year that the Economic Community of West African States was founded, through which West African countries manifested the will to partially put aside the barriers of colonial cultures imposed on the African continent. The Economic Community of West Africa States was instituted with the objective of promoting co-operation and integration in economic, social and cultural activities, eventually leading to the creation of an economic and monetary union through the integration of the national economies. The ultimate objective of all this is to raise the living standards of the peoples of the Community, promote and maintain economic stability, encourage cordial relations among Member States as an instrument of contributing to the development of the African Continent. However, the concomitant existence of a similar typically Francophone economic community such as the UEMOA confirms the continuity of the presence of this colonial cultural split in Africa, making Africa continue to be divided between Anglophone and Francophone parties.

The first problem emerges from the failure of Member States of the Community to concretely put into action the engagements and decisions taken during their regular meetings. The calendar of the ECOWAS economic programmes especially the common currency project have regularly been initially carried forward. The meetings and summits are the basis of the process, but they cannot exclusively progress regional integration. Conventions, resolutions and protocols are mostly adopted unanimously, but they only enter into vigour many years later, according to national ratification procedures that delay their adoption. Once published and implemented the collective action, regulations and procedures of the Community remain in the hands of national decision-makers, and sometimes are not followed by their timely implementation due to some limits imposed on them by the Constitutions of Member States.

Recent reforms marked by the restructuring of the main ECOWAS institutions, such as the transformation of the ECOWAS Secretariat to the ECOWAS Commission, the creation of the ECOWAS Parliament, the ECOWAS Bank for Investment and Development (EBID) and the ECOWAS Court of Justice, are constructive and encouraging developments aimed at promoting democracy, transparency and efficiency at both community level and at the level of individual Member States.

The ECOWAS realised that no economic integration and development is effective without culture and languages. Accordingly, it involved the African Academy of Languages in all of its activities relating to languages, in progressive partnership and cooperation. This awareness of the inevitable role of culture and/or languages in community development, is further symbolised by the fact that the ECOWAS has decided to embark on Cultural Industries as a form of Creative Enterprise, to institute a West African Cultural Institute (WACI), and in accordance with Article 62 (c) of the ECOWAS Treaty, to adopt a West African language as a working language in partnership with English, French and Portuguese.

The African Union has after its transformation aimed at accelerating the integration of the African continent in an atmosphere of peace and security and to defend a common position on issues concerning the continent in international relations. Good governance and democracy, which simply refer to respect for national constitutions, human rights and the rule of law, are fundamental to any form of socio-economic development. Lack of good governance and democracy engineer an atmosphere of conflict and instability, which renders impossible effective reconstruction. Therefore good governance and democracy that partly promote regional peace and security should continue to be the aim of the African Union. As the successor to the Organisation of African Unity, the African Union has been entrusted with greater power to remedy the defaults of African Nationalism and accelerate the process of integration, with a stronger commitment to democracy, good governance and human rights. The new African Union has created new institutions like the Pan-African Parliament,[159] the Economic, Social and Cultural Council, and the African Court of Justice,[160] (the principal judicial

---

[159] The Pan-African Parliament, one of the most important organs of the African Union, was inaugurated on Thursday, March 18, 2004. It has two hundred and two (202) legislators from 41 of the 53 Member States of the African Union.

[160] At the July 2008 African Union Summit, Justice Ministers formally adopted a single legal instrument to create an African Court of Justice and Human Rights. The 'Protocol on the Statute of the African Court of Justice and Human Rights' (the single Protocol) resulted from the merger of the African Court on Human and Peoples' Rights and the Court of Justice of the African Union. The decision to merge

organ of the Union with authority to rule on disputes over interpretation of AU treaties) and the African Central Bank (ACB), (one of the three financial institutions of the new African Union). The creation of the ACB, to be completed by 2028, was first initiated by the 1991 Abuja Treaty, but the 1999 Sirte Declaration envisaged accelerating the process. The ACB will take over the responsibilities of the African Monetary Fund over time. What is more encouraging about the transformation is that the AU has adopted a number of important innovative documents that aim at establishing norms at continental level, and reinforcing those already existing. For example the African Convention on Preventing and Combating Corruption (2003), the New Partnership for Africa's Development (NEPAD) and its associated Declaration on Democracy, Political, Economic and Corporate Governance, and the Africa Charter on Democracy, Elections and Governance (2007). These have demonstrated more pragmatism and dedication of the African people with regards to African unity. Only one African country has questioned its membership of the African Union. Morocco opposed the membership of Western Sahara as the Sahrawi Arab Democratic Republic and withdrew in 1984, when the majority of the Member States of the AU and the UN supported the Sahrawi National Polisario Front's Sahrawi Arab Democratic Republic.[161] The fact that Morocco protested the membership of the Sahrawi Arab Democratic Republic to the point of withdrawing from the Pan-African organisation, and continues to hold a special status within the African Union and to benefit from some of the services available to other Member States from the various institutions of the Organisation, shows the will and the good intention of the African people to go forward without rancour or discrimination to enhance its moves towards the African Renaissance. In fact delegates from Morocco usually participate at important negotiations of the African Union in an attempt to try to find lasting solution to the conflict. The AU continues to negotiate for a peaceful resolution of the problems affecting its Member States and indeed any African country.

---

the two courts at the Assembly of Heads of State and Government of the African Union in June 2004 was designed to ensure adequate resources to fund a single effective continental court.

[161] Morocco's ally, Zaire, similarly opposed the OAU's admission of the Sahrawi Arab Democratic Republic, and the Mobutu regime boycotted the organisation from 1984 to 1986.

The pragmatism of the new African Union is also demonstrated by the linking of culture and education in Africa by the Khartoum Declaration which equally created the African Academy of Languages (ACALAN) as its specialised institution, mandated to develop and promote African languages as a cultural and/or linguistic instrument of African integration and development. All this is empowered by the African Renaissance Campaign. Africa is therefore unmistakably on the right track and must continue moving forward.

Slavery dehumanised Africans while Colonialism exploited and deprived them from their resources before destroying their institutions and infrastructures. The trauma generated by these phenomena has handicapped Africa and led to lack of confidence and abandonment; but Africans must not stand indolently waiting for the others to take them out of marginalisation and precariousness. Africa must struggle on its own without helplessly depending on others. African reconstruction is a task for Africans first before being the duty of others. Therefore, Africans should continue to be more realistic, and cease being mere Nationalist figures, to become genuine Nationalists.

For that, a mechanism should be developed to strengthen and support the functioning of Pan-African institutions through the African Union, to better promote integration and render more autonomy and independence. African Nationalism should now neither conduce itself as Sub-Saharan or Mediterranean, nor as rich or poor. It should genuinely continue the process of African reconstruction for it to be sustainable, which can only be effective if the various hurdles that Africa is facing in this globalised world are successfully crossed or lifted, and they can, as we have noted, only be crossed or lifted by Africans themselves. But in this progressively more capitalistic and imperialistic world, the powers are defending their strategic interests and their efforts are liable to increasingly marginalise the continent.

Nationalism and reconstruction as presented by this work are therefore unrelenting socio-economic struggle and the total responsibility of Africans in which the adversaries are more or less omnipresent and unlikely ever to surrender. Africa should consequently no longer suffer from near-empty rhetoric and progress scepticism; and the average African must no longer be irresolute, and/or infirm of purpose. Africa has to march forward prudently

155

with pace, purpose, discipline and self-respect.

Bibliography

Primary sources

Personal interviews:

Personal interview.20 June 2007.
Personal interview. 15 July 2007.

Archives of the British government:

CAB 133/88 Meeting of Commonwealth Prime Ministers, London: Minutes and Papers, 1948
CAB 133/89 Meeting of Commonwealth Prime Ministers, London: Minutes and Papers, 1949
CAB 133/90 Meeting of Commonwealth Prime Ministers, London: Minutes and Papers, 1951
CAB 133/151 Prime Minister's visit to Africa, 1960: Minutes and Papers, 1959
CAB 133/252 Meeting of Commonwealth Prime Ministers: Minutes and Papers, 1962
CAB 133/253 Meeting of Commonwealth Prime Ministers: Minutes and Papers, 1964
CAB 133/220 Meeting of Commonwealth Officials, Meeting 1-9, 1st – 13th January 1965
CAB 133/342 Meeting of Commonwealth Prime Ministers: Papers A1 – 126, 17th August – 24 October 1966
CAB 133/384 Meeting of Commonwealth Prime Ministers, London: Papers B1 – B23, 16th December 1968 – 8th January 1969
CAB 133/385 Meeting of Commonwealth Prime Ministers, 1969: Papers C1 – C10, 11 December 1969 – 4th January 1969
CAB 164/4 Commonwealth Prime Ministers' Meeting, Lagos: Briefs for Harold Wilson, 1965 -1966
CO 537/4383 Congress of people against Imperialism, 1949
CO 537/6782 Communism in colonies: West Africa, 1951
CO 795/135/6 Colonial Development and Welfare Schemes, 1945-1946
CO 795/153/1 Colonial Development and Welfare Schemes: ten-year development programme for economic services and agriculture, 1947–1948
CO 859/135/2 Education Policy in Africa: Plans for Development in Colonies, 1948-1949
CO 879/35 War and Colonial Department and Colonial Office: Africa, Confidential Print: Nos. 411 to 418 and 421 to 422, 1642 – 1892

CO 1015/100 African Delegations to the Closer Association Conference, April 1952 in London: Brief for the April 1952 Conference, 1952
CO 1015/1661 Summary Paper on Future Constitutions in Colonies in Africa, 1957 – 1959
CO 1015/2515 Relationship between UN and British Colonial Territories, 1960
DO 35/9424 Dr Nkrumah's Declaration on Economic Imperialism, 1960
DO 121/215 Structure of the Commonwealth Future: Future of the Gold Coast, 1953 – 1954
DO 153/34 Commonwealth Prime Ministers' Meeting at Lagos: Discussions on Rhodesia, 1966
DO 183/13 Commonwealth Africa information PM conference in London, 1963
DO 207/87 Sanctions and Sanctions Evasions: Mandatory Sanctions Against Rhodesian Exports, 1966
DO 207/102 Organisation of African Unity (OAU) Discussions, 1966
FO 953/2296 UK action in event of country leaving the Commonwealth
FCO 49/74 Discussion with Commonwealth Secretariat on Membership of Commonwealth, 1967
PREM 11/1367 Independence of Gold Coast, 1952 – 1956

Archives of government of Ghana

Nkrumah's Address to the National Assembly, Accra, 25 November 1965 in Nkrumah, *Rhodesia File*, 103.
GPRL, BAA/RLAA/467, Speech by the Rt. Hon. Kwame Nkrumah, Prime Minister of Ghana, at the Opening Session of the Conference of Positive Action for Peace and Security in Africa on Thursday, 7th April 1960
All-African People''s Conference: Accra, 5th-13th December, 1958: Conference Resolution on Imperialism and Colonialism (Accra: Government Printers, [1958]), 9.

Archives of the Secretariat of the Commonwealth:

Address by Chief Emeka Anyaoku at CHOGM Opening Ceremony, Opening statement at a press conference given by the Commonwealth Secretary-General, Chief Emeka Anyaoku, 23 October 1997.
CS105/102/1 Press Extracts and Articles on the Secretary General and Commonwealth Secretariat, 1968.
C152/5/7 Commonwealth Prime Ministers' Conference, London, 1969: Documents – Circulated Papers.
CFMM 2006 Communiqué: Commonwealth Finance Ministers Meeting, Sri Lanka, Colombo 12-14 September 2006.

Final statement, International Conference on Small States and Economic Resilience organised by the Commonwealth Secretariat and the University of Malta at the Foundation for International Studies, Malta, 23-25 April 2007.

Report of the Commonwealth Observer Group – Nigeria State and Federal Elections of 14 and 21 April 2007.

Message by Commonwealth Secretary-General Don McKinnon on Commonwealth Day, London, 12 March 2007.

Networking for progress and prosperity: Report of the Commonwealth Secretary-General 2005, London, 20th October 2005.

PAD/C152/03/05 Commonwealth Prime Ministers Meeting: Record Copy of Papers, London, September 1966.

Report of a Round Table Meeting, *the Commonwealth and Democracy*, Session I, Cumberland Lodge, Windsor Great Park, 3-4 February 2000.

Report of the Commonwealth Secretary-General 2003, London, Commonwealth Secretariat, September 2003.

Speech by the Commonwealth Secretary-General Rt Hon Don McKinnon to the 51st Commonwealth Parliamentary Conference, Fiji Islands, 6 September 2005

Statement by Secretary-General Don McKinnon on World Day for Cultural Diversity for Dialogue and Development, 21 May 2007.

Archives of the Secretariat of the Francophonie

Charte de la Francophonie adoptée par la Conférence ministérielle de la Francophonie, Antananarivo, (Madagascar) le 23 novembre 2005.

Actes de la Xe Conférence des chefs d'État et de gouvernement des pays ayant le français en partage, Ouagadougou (Burkina Faso) 26-27 novembre 2004.

Actes de la IXe Conférence des chefs d'Etat et de gouvernement des pays ayant le français en partage Beyrouth, (Liban), 18, 19 et 20 octobre 2002.

Actes de la huitième Conférence des chefs d'Etat et de gouvernement des pays ayant le français en partage, Moncton (Canada-Nouveau-Brunswick), 3, 4 et 5 septembre 1999.

Actes de la septième Conférence des chefs d'Etat et de gouvernement des pays ayant le français en partage, Hanoi (Vietnam), 14, 15 et 16 novembre 1997.

Actes de la 21e session de la Conférence ministérielle de la Francophonie incluant la 24e session de la Conférence générale de l'Agence intergouvernementale de la Francophonie, Antananarivo (Madagascar), 22-23 novembre 2005.

Actes de la 19e session de la Conférence ministérielle de la Francophonie incluant la 23c session de la Conférence générale de l'Agence intergouvernementale de la Francophonie, Paris (France), 18-19 décembre 2003.

Actes de la 18e session de la Conférence ministérielle de la Francophonie incluant la 22e session de la Conférence générale de l'Agence intergouvernementale de la Francophonie, Lausanne (Suisse), 12-13 décembre 2002.

Actes de la XIIIe Conférence ministérielle de la Francophonie, Moncton (Canada-Nouveau-Brunswick), 31 août et 1er septembre 1999.

Déclaration de Bucarest (29 septembre 2006) - XIe Conférence des chefs d'État et de gouvernement des pays ayant le français en partage, l28 et 29 septembre 2006.

Déclaration de Ouagadougou (27 novembre 2004) - Xe Conférence des chefs d'Etat et de gouvernement des pays ayant le français en partage, 26 et 27 novembre 2004.

Rapport du Secrétaire général de la Francophonie. *Solidarité et développement durable* 2004- 2006, septembre 2006.

Archives of the African Union

CIAS/PLEN.2/REV.2 / A – F CIAS/Plen.3 / A – C CIAS/RES.1/REV.1 / IAS/Res.1/Rev.1 / CIAS/Res.2 Resolution adopted by the first conference of independent African heads of state and government held in Addis Ababa, Ethiopia, 22 – 25 May 1963.

AHG/Res. 1 (1) - AHG/Res. 24 (1) Resolution adopted by the first conference of independent African heads of state and government held in Cairo, UAR,17 - 21 July 1964.

AHG/Res. 25 (II) - AHG/Res. 45 (II) Resolution adopted by the second ordinary session of the Assembly of Heads of state and government held in Accra, Ghana 21 – 26 October 1965.

AHG/Res. 46 (III) - AHG/Res. 48 (III) Resolution adopted by the third ordinary session of the Assembly of Heads of state and government held in Addis Ababa, Ethiopia, 5 - 9 November 1966.

AHG/Res. 104 (XIX) Resolution on Western Sahara, assembly of heads of state and government, Nineteenth Ordinary Session 6 – 12 June 1983 Addis Ababa, Ethiopia.

AHG/Res. 111 (XIX) Resolution on the policy of destabilisation by racist South African regime against Southern African Independent States, Assembly of Heads of state and government, Nineteenth Ordinary Session 6 – 12 June 1983 Addis Ababa, Ethiopia.

AHG/Res. 112 (XIX) Resolution on South Africa, assembly of heads of state and government, Nineteenth Ordinary Session 6 – 12 June 1983 Addis Ababa, Ethiopia.

AHG/Res. 113 (XIX) Resolution on the African candidatures to international organisations, Assembly of heads of state and government, Nineteenth Ordinary Session 6 – 12 June 1983 Addis Ababa, Ethiopia.

AHG/Res. 115 (XIX) Resolution on the Lagos Plan of Action and the Final Act of Lagos, Assembly of Heads of state and government, Nineteenth Ordinary Session 6 – 12 June 1983 Addis Ababa, Ethiopia.

AHG/Res.130 (XIX) Resolution on the Establishment of a Special Fund for Africa, Assembly of head of state and government, Twentieth Ordinary Session 12 – 15 November 1984 Addis Ababa, Ethiopia.

AHG/Res.131 (XIX) Resolution on the Inter-African Economic Co-operation and Integration, Assembly of head of state and government, Twentieth Ordinary Session 12 – 15 November 1984 Addis Ababa, Ethiopia.

AHG/Res.190 (XXVI) Resolution on the Establishment of the African Economic Community, Assembly of head of state and government, Twenty-sixth Ordinary Session 9 – 11 July 1990 Addis Ababa, Ethiopia.

AHG/Res.198 (XXVI) Resolution on the African Commission on Human and Peoples' Rights, Assembly of head of state and government, Twenty-sixth Ordinary Session 9 – 11 July 1990 Addis Ababa, Ethiopia.

AHG/Decl.1. (XXVIII) Decision on a Mechanism for Conflict Prevention, Management and Resolution, Assembly of head of state and government, Twenty-eighth Ordinary Session 29 June – 1 July 1992.

Assembly/AU/Dec.95 (VI) Decision on the Statutes of the African Academy of Languages (ACALAN).

Decision CM/Dec. 613 (LXXIV) of Lusaka related to the establishment of the African Academy of Languages.

AHG/Decl.2 (XXXVI)Lome Declaration, Assembly of head of state and government, Thirty-Sixth Ordinary Session/Fourth Ordinary Session of the African Economic Community 10-12 July, 2000 Lome, Togo.

AHG/Decl.5 (XXXVI)Declaration on the Framework for an OAU response to unconstitutional changes of government, Assembly of head of state and government, Thirty-Sixth Ordinary Session/Fourth Ordinary Session of the African Economic Community 10-12 July, 2000 Lome, Togo.

AHG/Dec.143 (XXXVI)Decision on the establishment of the African Union and the Pan-African Parliament, Assembly of head of state and government,Thirty-Sixth Ordinary Session/Fourth Ordinary Session of the African Economic Community 10-12 July, 2000 Lome, Togo.

AHG/Dec.150 (XXXVI)Decision on unconstitutional changes of government in Africa - CM/2166 (LXXII) Assembly of head of state and government,Thirty-Sixth Ordinary Session/Fourth Ordinary Session of the African Economic Community 10-12 July, 2000 Lome, Togo.

AHG/Dec.1 (XXXVII) Decision on the Implementation of the Sirte Summit Decision on the African Union, Assembly of head of state and government,Thirty-seventh Ordinary Session/Fifth Ordinary Session of the AEC 9 – 11 July, 2001 Lusaka, Zambia.

AHG/Decl.1 (XXXVII) Declaration on the New Common Initiative (MAP and OMEGA), Assembly of head of state and government,Thirty-seventh Ordinary Session/Fifth Ordinary Session of the AEC 9 – 11 July, 2001 Lusaka, Zambia.

Assembly/AU/Dec.17 (II) Decision on the Protocol to the Treaty Establishing the African Economic Community Relating to the Pan-African Parliament, Assembly of the African Union, Second Ordinary Session 10 - 12 July 2003 Maputo, Mozambique.

Ext/Assembly/AU/Dec.2 (II) Decision on a Non-aggression and common defence pact, Assembly of the African Union, 2nd Extraordinary Session 27 - 28 February 2004 Sirte, Libya.

Assembly/AU/Dec.83 (V) Decision on the Merger of the African Court on Human and Peoples' Rights and the Court of Justice of the African Union – (Doc. Assembly/AU/6 (V)), Assembly of the African Union, Fifth Ordinary Session 4 – 5 July 2005 Sirte, Libya.

Assembly/AU/Decl. 2 (V) Sirte Declaration on the Reform of the United Nations, Assembly of the African Union, Fifth Ordinary Session 4 – 5 July 2005 Sirte, Libya.

Assembly/AU/Resolution.1 (V) Resolution on the United Nations Reform: Security Council Assembly of the African Union, Fifth Ordinary Session 4 – 5 July 2005 Sirte, Libya.

Assembly/AU/Dec.166 (IX) Decision on the Protocol on Relations between the African Union and the Regional Economic Communities (RECs) - Doc. EX.CL/348 (IX) Assembly of the African Union, Ninth Ordinary Council 1 – 3 July 2007 Accra, Ghana.

Archives of the Economic Community of West African States

Treaty of the Economic Community of West African States (ECOWAS), 28 May, 1975, Lagos, Nigeria.

Revised Treaty of the Economic Community of West African States (ECOWAS), 24 July, 1993, Cotonou, Benin.

A/SP1/12/01 Protocol on Democracy and Good Governance. Supplementary to the Protocol relating to the Mechanism for Conflict Prevention, Management, Resolution, Peacekeeping and Security, 21 December 2001, Dakar, Senegal.

Protocol Relating to the Application of Compensation Procedures for Loss of Revenue Incurred by ECOWAS Member States as a Result of Trade Liberalisation Scheme, May 2002, Yamoussokro, Cote d'Ivoire.

Protocol Relating to the Mechanism for Conflict Prevention, Management, Resolution, Peace-keeping and Security, 10 December, 1999, Lome, Togo.

A/SP.1/7/86 Supplementary Protocol on the Second Phase (Right of Establishment) of the Protocol on Free Movement of Persons, Right of Residence and Establishment, 01 July, 1986, Abuja, Nigeria.

A/SP.2/5/90 Supplementary Protocol on the Implementation of the Third Phase (Right of Establishment) of the Protocol on Free Movement of Persons, Right of Residence and Establishment, 30 May, 1990, Banjul, The Gambia.

A/SP.1/7/85 Supplementary Protocol on the Code of Conduct for the Implementation of the Protocol on Free Movement of Persons, Right of Residence and Establishment, 06 July, 1985, Lome, Togo

A/P.1/5/79 Protocol Relating to the Free Movement of Persons, Residence and Establishment, 29 May, 1979, Dakar, Senegal.

Protocol Relating to the Fund for Co-operation, Compensation and Development of the Economic Community of West African States, 05 November, 1976, Lome, Togo.

Protocol on the Assessment of the Loss of Revenue by Member States, 05 November, 1976, Lome, Togo.

Autobiographies and books written by politicians:

Atlee, Clement. *Empire to Commonwealth*, London: Oxford University Press, 1961

Cohen A.B. *British Policy in Changing Africa*, London: Routledge and Kegan Paul, 1959.

Gordon-Walker P. *The Commonwealth, London*: Secker and Warburg, 1962.

Lugard, Lord. *The Dual Mandate in British Tropical Africa*, (1922), London: Frank Cass, 1965.

Macmillan W.M. *The Road to Self Rule: A study in Colonial Evolution*, Londres: Faber and Faber, 1959.

Wilson Harold. *The Labour Government 1964 – 1970, a Personal Record*, London: Weidenfield and Nicholson, 1971.

Secondary sources

Books
A.

Achebe, Chinua. *A Man of the People*, New York : Anchor Books, 1989.

Achebe, Chinua. *The Trouble with Nigeria*. London: Heinemann, 1983.

Achebe, Chinua. *Things Fall Apart*. London: Penguin Books Ltd, 2001.

American Society of African Culture ed. Pan-Africanism Reconsidered–orgname, Berkeley, CA. University of California Press, 1962.

Anderson, Benedict. *Imagined Communities: Reflections on the Origin and Spread of Nationalism*.rev. ed. NY: Verso, 1991.

Ajayi, J. F. A., Crowder, M. *History of West Africa*, London, Longman, 1971.

Ashcroft, Bill, Gareth Griffiths & Helen Tiffin, *The Empire Writes Back: Theory and*

Practice in Post-Colonial Literatures. NY: Routledge, 1989.

Ayandele, E. A. *African Historical Studies*, London, Frank Cass, 1979.

Arthur de Gobineau, Joseph. *Essai sur l'inégalité des races humaines*, Paris : Librairie de Paris, 1933.

Appiah, Kwame Anthony. *In My Father's House: Africa in the Philosophy of Culture.* New York: Oxford University Press, 1992.

B.

Bâ, Sylvia Washington. *The Concept of Negritude in the Poetry of Léopold Sédar Senghor.* Princeton, New Jersey: Princeton University Press, 1973.

BernabeJean, Chamoiseau Patrick ; et al. *Éloge de la créolité = In praise of Creoleness*, Paris: Gallimard, 1997.

Boahen, A. Adu. *African Perspectives on Colonialism*, Baltimore: John Hopkins Press, 1987.

Boahen, A. Adu. *Topics in West Africa History*, Essex, Longman, 1981.

Bezenguissa, Rémy et Nantet, Bernard. *L'Afrique : mythes et réalités d'un continent.* Paris: Le cherche midi éditeur, 1995.

Boahen A. Adu, dir. *Histoire générale de l'Afrique, volume VII : L'Afrique sous domination coloniale, 1880-1935*, Paris : UNESCO, 1987.

Boahen, A. Adu. *African Perspectives on Colonialism.* Baltimore: Johns Hopkins University Press, 1989.

Boahen A.A. and Tidy M. Webster, J.B. *The Growth of African Civilisation: The Revolutionary Years: West Africa since 1800*, Essex: Longman.

Breuilly, John. 1982. Nationalism and the State. ISBN 0-312-56005-2.

Burke, Edmund. *On Empire, Liberty and Reform: Speeches and Letters.* Ed. David Bromwich. New Haven: Yale University Press, 2000.

Bute, E L, Harmer, H J P. *The Black Handbook: The People, History and Politics of African Diaspora.* London: Cassell, 1997.

C.

Ceesay, Amadou, ed. *Africa and Europe: from partition to independence or dependence.*London: Croom Helm, cop, 1986.

Césaire Aimé, *Cahier d'un retour au pays natal*, Paris : Présence africaine, 1983.

Chinweizu, Onwuchekwa Jemie, Ihechukwu Madubuike. *Toward the Decolonization of African Literature.* Washington, D.C.: Howard University Press, 1983.

Condé, Maryse. *En attendant le bonheur (Heremakonon) : roman*, Paris : Seghers, 1988.

Connah, Graham. *African civilisations: pre-colonial cities and states in tropical Africa, an archaeological perspective.* Cambridge: Cambridge University Press, 1987.

Cornevin, Robert. *Histoire de l'Afrique: colonisation, décolonisation, indépendance.*Paris : Payot, 1975.

Crowder, M. *The Cambridge History of Africa*, vol. 8, Cambridge, Cambridge University Press, 1984.

Crowder, Michael. *West Africa: An Introduction to its History.* Essex: Longman Group, 1977.

D.

Darwin, Charles. *The Origin of Species*, London: Gramercy Books; new edition 1995.

Davidson, Basil. *Africa in modern history: the search for a new society*. London: Allen Lane, 1978.

Davidson, Basil. *Africa in history*. London: Wiedenfeld and Nicolson, 1968.

Davidson, Basil. *Africa: History of a continent*, London, Spring Books, 1972.

Davidson, Basil. *The Growth of African Civilisation. A History of West Africa 1000-1800*, London, Longman, 1965. .

Davidson, Basil. *Modern Africa: A Social and Political History*.New York: Longman, 1994.

Deniau, Jean-François. *La francophonie*, Paris : Presses universitaires de France, 1983 Dickson, A Mungazi. *The Mind of Black Africa*. Connecticut: Westport, 1996.

Diouf, Mamadou. *Le clientélisme, la « technocratie » et après »,Sénégal Trajectoire d'un État*, Paris, Dakar : Karthala/Cordesria, 1992.

Du Bois, W. E. B. *The Autobiography of W. E. B. DuBois*. New York: International, 1968.

Du Bois W.E.B. *The Souls of Black Folk*, New York: Penguin. April 1996.

Durgnan Grann, Henry Lewis, Peter. *Colonialism in Africa: 1870-1960*. Cambridge: Cambridge University Press, 1969-1975. 5Vol.

E.

Esedebe, P. Olisanwuche. *Pan-Africanism: The Idea and Movement, 1776–1963*, Washington, D.C.: Howard University Press, 1982.

F.

Fage, Cliver et John Donnelly, Rolland. *The Cambridge History of Africa*. Cambridge, London, New York, NY: Cambridge University Press, 1975.

Fage J D. *A History of West Africa: An Introductory Survey*. Cambridge: Cambridge University Press, 1955, 1969.

Fanon Frantz. *Les damnés de la terre*, Paris : Éditions la Découverte, 1968.

Fanon, Frantz. *Peau Noire Masques Blancs*, Paris: Seuil, 1968.

Ferro, Marc ed. *Le livre noire du Colonialisme XVIe – XXIe siècle : de l'extermination à la repentance*, Paris, éditions Robert Laffont, 2003.

G.

Gailey, Harry A. *Historical Dictionary of the Gambia*. N J & London: Scarecrow Press, 1987.

Gandhi, Leela. *Postcolonial Theory: A Critical Introduction*. New York: Columbia University Press, 1988.

Geiss, Imanuel. *The pan-African movement; a history of pan-Africanism in America, Europe, and Africa*, New York, Africana Pub. Co. 1974.

Gellar, Sheldon. *Senegal: An African nation between Islam and the West*. Boulder, CO: Westview Press, 1982.

Gellner, Ernest. *Nations and Nationalism*, NY: Cornell University Press, 1983.

Gordon, April A. and Donald L. Gordon, eds. *Understanding Contemporary Africa.* 2nd ed. Boulder, CO: Lynne Rienner Publishers, 1996.

Godfrey, James et al. *Commonwealth Perspectives*.Durham, NC: Duke University Press, 1958.

Guibernau, Montserrat, *Nationalism: The Nation-State and Nationalism in the Twentieth Century*, Cambridge: Polity Press, 1996.

H.

Hargreaves, John D. *Prelude to the Partition of West Africa.* London: Macmillan & Co LTD, 1963.

Hargreaves, John D. *Decolonization in Africa*, London: Longman Group UK. 1990.

Hegel Friedrich et al; et al.*La phenomologie de l'esprit de Hegel*, Bruxelles: Revue internationale de philosophie, 2007.Hesseling, Gerti. *Histoire Politique du Sénégal: Institution, Droit et Société*.Paris: Karthala et ASC,1985.

Hobsbawm, E.J., *Nations and Nationalism since 1780: Programme, Myth, Reality.* NY: Columbia UP, 1990.

Hodgkin, Thomas. *Nationalism in Colonial Africa.* New York: New York University Press, 1957.

Huntington, Samuel P. *Political Order in Changing Society.* New Haven and London, Yale University Press, 1968.

J.

J. Ayodele Langley, *Pan-Africanism and Nationalism in West Africa, 1900-1945; a study in ideology and social classes,*Oxford, Clarendon Press, 1973.

Jean-Paul Sartre. *"Black Orpheus,""What Is Literature?"and Other Essays* Cambridge: Harvard University Press, 1988.

Jeyifo Biodum, Soyinka Wole.*Conversations with Wole Soyinka*, Jackson : University Press of Mississippi, 2001.

K.

Kennedy, Paul. *The Rise and fall of Great Powers*, London: Fontana Press, 1988.

Kitchen, Lexington, Helen, Mass, ed. *Africa: from mystery to maze.* Toronto: Lexington books, 1978.

Killingray, David. *Africa and the Second World War.* London: Macmillan, 1986.

Kent, John. *The internalization of Colonialism: Britain, France and Black Africa.* 1939-1956. Oxford: Oxford University Press, 1992.

King Martin Luther Jr. *Why We Can't Wait*, UK, Penguin, 1991.

L.

Lancaster, Carol. *So Much To Do, So Little Done*, Chicago: University of Chicago Press, 1999.

Langley, J. Ayodele. *Pan-Africanism and Nationalism in West Africa, 1900-1945* (London: Oxford University Press, 1973).

Legum, Colin. *Pan-Africanism: A Short Political Guide*, New York: Frederick A. Praeger, 1962.

Loomba, Ania. *Colonialism/postColonialism*. London, New York: Routledge, 1998.

Lawrence, James. *The savage wars: British campaigns in Africa, 1870-1920*. London: Robert Hale, 1985.

Lugan, Bernard. *Afrique, bilan de la colonisation*. Paris : Perrin, 1991.

Lugan, Bernard. *Afrique: de la colonisation philanthropique à la recolonisation humanitaire,* Paris : Christian de Bartillat, 1995.

Lee, Loyde E. *World War II in Europe, Africa and the Americas, with general sources: a handbook of literature and research.* London: Greenwood, 1997.

M.

Macmillan, W. M. *Africa emergent*. London: Faber and Faber, 1938.

Marshall, P.J. ed. *The Cambridge Illustrated History of the British Empire*, Cambridge: Cambridge University Press, 1996.

Mazrui, Ali A. *The Africans: A Triple Heritage.* Boston: Little Brown & Co. 1986.

Mazrui, Ali. *The African Condition.* New York, Cambridge University Press. 1980.

Mehta, Uday. *Liberalism and Empire: A Study in Nineteenth-Century British Liberal Thought.* Chicago: University of Chicago Press, 1999.

Milne, June. *Kwame Nkrumah: A Biography*, London, PANAF, 1999.

Morrison, Donald George. *Black Africa: a comparative handbook 2ed.* New York: Paragon House, 1989.

Mungazi, Dickson A. *The Mind of Black Africa.* Connecticut: Westport, 1996.

Munro, J.Forbes. *Britain in Tropical Africa: 1880-1960. Economic Relationships and Impact.* London: Macmillan, 1984.

N.

Nations-Unies. *Rapport mondial sur le développement humain*, PNUD, Paris, Economica, 1991.

Ndegwa, Philip. *Africa's development crisis.* London: Heinemann, 1988.

Ngugi wa Thiong'o. *Decolonising the Mind: The Politics of Language in African Literature.* London: J. Currey; Portsmouth, N.H.: Heinemann, 1986.

Ngugi wa Thiong'o. *Moving the Centre: The Struggle for Cultural Freedoms.* London: J. Currey; Portsmouth, N.H.: Heinemann, 1993.

Nkrumah Kwme. *Axioms Kwame Nkrumah: The Freedom Fighters' Edition.* London: Panaf, 1967.

Nkurumah, Kwame. *Towards colonial freedom: Africa in the struggle against world Imperialism.* London: Panaf, 1979.

Nkurumah, Kwame. *Class struggle in Africa.* London: Panaf, 1970.

Nkrumah, Kwame. *I Speak of Freedom*, London: Heinemann, 1961.

Nkrumah, Kwame. *Africa Must Unite.* London: Heinemann, 1964.

Nkrumah, Kwame. *Neo Colonialism: The Last Stage of Imperialism*, London: Heinemann, 1965.

Nkrumah, Kwame. *Challenge of the Congo. A Case Study of Foreign Pressures in an Independent State*, London: Panaf, 1966.

Nkrumah, Kwame. *Handbook of Revolutionary Warfare*, London: Panaf, 1968.

Nkrumah, Kwame. *Revolutionary Path*, London: Panaf, 1973.

Nkrumah, Kwame. *The Spectre of Black Power, in The Struggle Continues*, London: Panaf, 1980.

Nyang, Sulayman Sheih. *Islam, Christianity, and African Identity*. Brattleboro, VT: Amana Books, 1984.

O.

Oliver, Roland Anthony. *Africa in the Iron Age: C. 500 BC to AD 1400*. Cambridge, London, New York: Cambridge University Press, 1975.

Osei Akwasi P. *Ghana: recurrence and change in post-independence African state*. New York: Peter Lang, 1999.

Owusu-Ansah, David and Mcfarland, Daniel Miles. *Historical Dictionary of Ghana*. N J & London: the Scarecrow Press, 1995.

P.

Padmore, George. *Pan-Africanism or Communism? The Coming Struggle*. London: Dennis Dobson, 1956.

Pearce, R O. *The turning point in Africa: British colonial policy 1938-48*. London, New Jersey: Frank Cass. 1983.

Praeger, Michèle. *The imaginary Caribbean and Caribbean imaginary*, Lincoln : University of Nebraska Press, 2003.

Pitts, Jennifer. 2005. *A Turn Toward Empire: The Rise of Imperial Liberalism in Britain and France*. Princeton and Oxford: Princeton University Press.

Porter, Bernard. *The Lion's Share: Short History of British Imperialism 1850-1995*, 3rd edition, London: Longman, 1996.

R.

Ravenhill, John. *Africa in Economic Crisis*. London: Macmillan, 1986.

Reader, John. *Africa: A Biography of the Continent*. London: Hamish Hamilton, 1997.

Rice, Berkley. *Enter Gambia: the birth of an improbable nation*. Boston: Houghton Mifflin, 1967

Rodney, Walter. *How Europe underdeveloped Africa*, Washington D.C.: Howard University Press, 1982.

Roland, Oliver, and Michael Crowder, gen. eds. *The Cambridge Encyclopedia of Africa*. Cambridge, UK: New York: Cambridge University Press, 1981. .

Ross, George. *Back to Africa: George Ross and the Maroons, from Nova Scotch to Sierra Leone*. Trenton NJ: Africa World, 1994.

Rotberg, Irwin, Al'Amin, Robert, Mazrui, Ali. *Protest and power in black Africa*. New York: Oxford University Press, 1970.

Royle, Trevor. *Winds of Change: The end of Empire in Africa*. London: John Murray, 1996.

Rugand John. *The Burdens*. Nairobi, London, New York: Oxford University Press, 1972.

S.

Sartre, Jean-Paul. *Orphée noire,* Paris : Présence africaine, 1972.

Seba, Mark. *Contact languages : pidgins and Creoles.* New York: Saint Martin Press INC, 1997.

Senghor, Léopold Sédar. Aziza, Mohamed.*La poesie de l'action. Conversations avec Mohamed Aziza,* Stock, Paris, 1980.

Senghor, Léopold Sédar. *Anthologie de la Nouvelle poésie nègre et malgache de la langue française,* Paris, Presse universitaire de France, 1969.

Senghor, Léopold Sédar. *Anthologie de la nouvelle poésie nègre et malgache de langue française,* Paris : PUF, 5ᵉ édition, 2002.

Senghor, Léopold Sédar. *Liberté 1. Négritude et humanisme,* Paris : Seuil, 1964.

Senghor, Léopold Sédar. *Liberté 1. Nation et voie africaine du socialisme,* Paris : Seuil, 1971.Senghor, Léopold Sédar. *Négritude et civilisation de l'universel,* Paris : Seuil, 1977.

Sorel, Jacqueline. *Léopold Sédar Senghor: L'émotion et la raison,* Paris : Sepia, 1995.

Soyinka, Wole. *The Burden of Memory, the Muse of Forgiveness,* Oxford: Oxford University Press, 2000.

Soyinka, Wole. *Myth, Literature, and the African World,* Cambridge, New York : Cambridge University Press, 1976.

Spleth, Janice. *Léopold Sédar Senghor,* Boston: Twayne publishers, 1985.

T.

Tomlinson, John, *Cultural Imperialism: A Critical Introduction,* Baltimore: The Johns Hopkins University Press, 1991.

Touré, S., *Expérience guinéenne et Unité Africaine,* Paris, Présence Africaine, 1960.

Thompson, V. Bakpetu. *Africa and Unity: The Evolution of Pan-Africanism* (London: Longman, 1969).

Thornton, John L. *Africa and Africans in the making of the Atlantic world: 1400-1800* 2ⁿᵈ ed.Cambridge, MA: Cambridge University Press, 1998.

Tocqueville, Alexis. *Writings on Empire and Slavery.* ed. and trans. Jennifer Pitts. Baltimore, MD: Johns Hopkins University Press.

Traoré, Aminata. *Le Viol de l'imaginaire,* Paris : Actes Sud-Fayard, 2002.

V.

Van Sertima, Ivan, ed. *Cheikh Anta Diop.* Great African Thinkers Series, v. 1. New Brunswick, NH: Transaction Books, 1986.

Van Sertima, Ivan, ed. *Great Black Leaders: Ancient and Modern.* New Brunswick, NJ: Journal of African Civilizations, 1988.

V. Bakpetu Thompson, *Africa and Unity: The Evolution of Pan-Africanism,* New York: Humanities Press, 1969.

W.

Walker, Conner. *Beyond Reason: The Nature of the Ethnonational Bond.* in *EthnoNationalism: The Quest for Understanding.* Princeton, Princeton, University Press, 1994.

Wallerstein, Immanuel. *The Modern World System,* 3 vols. New York: Academic Press, 1989.

Wollstonecraft, Mary. *A vindication of the rights of women,* [2nd ed.], Farnborough : Gregg, 1970. .

Woolf, Stuart, ed. *Nationalism in Europe 1815 to the present: A Reader.* NY: Routledge, 1996.

Wright, S. Okolo, J. eds., *West Africa: Regional Cooperation and Development,* *Boulder,* Westview Press 1990.

Y.

Young, Robert, *Colonial Desire: Hybridity in Theory, Culture and Race,* NY: Routledge, 1995.

Periodicals

Beck, Linda J., Senegal's "Patrimonial Democrats : Incremental Reform and Obstacles to the Consolidation of Democracy", Canadian Journal Of African Studies, Vol. 31, no1, (1997): 25.

Ben Yahmed, Marwane, Soudan François. *"Les vérités d'Obasanjo",* *Jeune Afrique l'intelligent,* n° 2316, (mai – juin 2005) : 43 – 45.

Colette, Elise. *"L'Afrique est une priorité",* Jeune Afrique l'intelligent, n° 2198.43ᵉ année, (février – mars 2003) : 64.

Conde Maaryse, *"Négritude césairienne, Négritude senghorienne."* Revue de littérature comparée 3.4 (juillet-décembre 1974): 409-419. (P413)

Constantin, F. Constantin, B., *"Perspectives africaines et bouleversements internationaux",* Politique Africaine, "l'Afrique autrement", n°39 (février 1990) : 59.

Nyang, Sulayman S. "Ten Years of Gambia's Independence: A Political Analysis." *Presence Africaine* n°104 (1977): 29 - 43.

Péroncel-Hugoz, Jean Pierre. *"Léopold Sédar Senghor l'euronègre",* Jeune Afrique, hors série n° 11, (2006): 24 – 29.

P. O. Esedebe, "Origins and Meanings of Pan-Africanism," *Presence Africaine,* 73 (First Quarter, 1970).

Silla, Ousman. *"L'évolution Politique de la Gambie."* Revue française d'études politiques africaines n°25 (janvier 1968) : 65 – 73.

Thorin, Valérie. *"Abdou Diouf : Senghor, le Sénégal et moi",* Jeune Afrique, hors série n° 11, (2006): 102 – 107.

Ukapi, S C. "Gambia: Independence and after." Africa Quarterly n°14 (1972): 340 - 352.

Mortimer, Mildred P. "Sine and Seine: The Quest for Synthesis in Senghor's Life and Poetry." Research in African Literatures, Volume 33, Number 4, Winter 2002: 38-50

Web pages

Encyclopaedia Britannica, "talion" 12 Oct. 2012.
<http://www.britannica.com/EBchecked/topic/581485/talion>
Nkrumah and the Pan-African Centered Perspective. "Speech at the opening
of the Institute of African Studies, Legon, 25 Oct. 1963". 10 Oct 2012.
<http://www.nkrumah.net/lit-review/litrvw6-primarysrc-10.html>
Organisation of African Unity. "OAU Charter." 11 Dec. 2010. 15 Nov.
2012.
<http://www.au.int/en/sites/default/files/OAU_Charter_1963_0.pdf>
African Union. "Constitutive Act." 06 Jun. 2010. 9 Oct. 2012.
<http://www.africa-
union.org/root/au/aboutau/constitutive_act_en.htm>
ECOWAS. "Treaty of ECOWAS". 2007. 20 may 2012.
<http://www.comm.ecowas.int/sec/index.php?id=treaty&lang=en
The   Commission   for   Africa.<
http://www.commissionforafrica.info/articles>
The Commonwealth. "Harare Commonwealth Declaration." Harare,
Zimbabwe 20 Oct. 1991. 13 May 2012.
<http://www.thecommonwealth.org/document/34293/35468/35773/hara
re.htm>
The Commonwealth. "Declaration of Commonwealth Principles, 1971",
Singapore. 22 January 1971. 10 Sept. 2012.
<http://www.thecommonwealth.org/Templates/Internal.asp?NodeID=32
987>
The National Archives, UK. "The Cabinet Papers 1915 – 1982: Dominion
status   and   legislation."   05.   Jan.   2012.
<http://www.nationalarchives.gov.uk/cabinetpapers/themes/dominion-
status-legislation.htm>
The Pan-African movement. "5th Pan African Congress – United Kingdom
– 1945". 10 May 2012.
<http://www.pan-africanmovement.net/2012/01/18/5th-pan-african-
congress-united-kingdom-1945/>.
Tine, Antoine. "Léopold Sédar Senghor et Chiek Anta Diop face au
panafricanisme." Papier présenté lors du colloque 30ème anniversaire du
CODESRIA 51973 - 2003), Dakar, 10 – 12 déc. 2003.
<http://www.codesria.org/links/conférences/dakar/tine.pdf>
Irish Abroad. "Ugandan dictator's plane was forbidden to land." 2009.10Feb
2012.
<http://www.irishabroad.com/news/irishpost/news/ArchiveSecretsUnloc
ked050108.asp>
Columbia   encyclopedia.   "Nationalism".   15   Feb   2012.
<http://www.encyclopedia.com/searchresults.aspx?q=Nationalism>
Encyclopedia Britannica "Talion". 15 Feb. 2012.

171

<http://www.britannica.com/EBchecked/topic/581485/talion>
Encyclopedia Britannica. "Black History: Negritude". 10 Oct. 2012.
<http://www.britannica.com/blackhistory>
Severusa, Septimius "Nkrumah: The untold story", 10 Apr. 2012:
<http://ghanaian-chronicle.com/nkrumah-the-untold-story/>
"Negritude."10 Apr. 2012.
<http://muse.jhu.edu/login?auth=0&type=summary&url=/journals/resear
ch_in_african_literatures/v033/33.4mortimer.pdf>
African Reparation Movement,
<http://www.arm.arc.co.uk/legalBasis.html>
"Africa Population 2014."
<https://africacheck.org/reports/how-many-countries-in-africa-how-hard-
can-the-question-be/>
La Francophonie. "Une Histoire de la Francophonie."
<http://www.francophonie.org/Une-histoire-de-la-Francophonie.html>
Ghana Business and Finance. "The ECO: a common currency phantasm or
certainty?"   <http://www.ghanabizmedia.com/ghanabizmedia/january-
2011-ecowas/191-the-eco-a-common-currency-phantasm-or-
certainty.html>

Online newspapers
Brogan, Benedict. "It's time to celebrate the Empire, says Brown." Daily
Mail.15 January 2005. 25 April 2014.
<http://www.dailymail.co.uk/news/article-334208/Its-time-celebrate-
Empire-says-Brown.html>
Mbaye, Sanou. *"En finir avec la dépendance : Souhaitable union des économies
africaines"*, *Le Monde diplomatique*, septembre 1995. 13 Sept. 2012.
<http://www.monde-diplomatique.fr/1995/09/MBAYE/1731>.
Lacouture, Jean. *"Bandung ou la fin de l'ère coloniale."* Avril 2005. 25 Jul. 2012.
<http://www.monde-diplomatique.fr/2005/04/LACOUTURE/12062>
BBC News. "UK regrets The Gambia's withdrawal from Commonwealth." 3 Oct. 2013.
14 May 2014.
<http://www.bbc.com/news/uk-24376127>
Sky News. "Commonwealth 'Relief' Over Gambia Withdrawal." 03 Oct
2013. 14 May 2014.
<http://news.sky.com/story/1149799/commonwealth-relief-over-gambia-
withdrawal>
Vanguard (Lagos) "WABA Explains Collapse of Ecowas Travellers Cheque." 17 Aug.
2002. 11 Oct. 2012.
<http://www.modernghana.com/news/25126/1/waba-explains-collapse-
of-ecowas-travellers-cheque.html>

Online books.

Adewuni, Salawu. "West African Nationalism Rediscovered." 08 Oct. 2012.<http://www2.carleton.ca/africanstudies/ccms/wp-content/ccms-files/West- African-Nationalism-rediscovered.pdf>

Chief Emeka Anyaoku. "Interview with Guy Harrison", the Caymanian Compass newspaper (Cayman Islands) 01 Oct. 2012. <http://peaceguy.8m.com/photo2.html>

Kohn, Magaret. "Colonialism", Stanford encyclopedia of philosophy, 9 May 2012. <http://plato.stanford.edu/entries/Colonialism/>

CDROM

Blondy Alpha, "*Ça me fait mal*," *Masada*. Universal, 1992. CD

Index

177

www.ingramcontent.com/pod-product-compliance
Lightning Source LLC
Chambersburg PA
CBHW062204280526

45788CB00001B/437

* 9 7 8 1 5 2 3 7 9 2 9 5 5 *